D. C.).

Pekingese

Everything about Purchase, Care, Nutrition,
Breeding, Behavior, and Training

With 47 Color Photographs

Illustrations by Michele Earle-Bridges

BARRON'S

About the Author

Caroline Coile is an award-winning author who has written articles about dogs for both scientific and lay publications. She holds a Ph.D. in the field of neuroscience and behavior, with special interests in canine sensory systems, genetics, and behavior. Her own dogs have been nationally ranked in conformation, obedience, and field-trial competition.

All inquiries should be addressed to:
Barron's Educational Series, Inc.
250 Wireless Boulevard
Hauppauge, NY 11788

International Standard Book No. 0-8120-9676-2

Library of Congress Catalog Card No. 96-1967

Library of Congress Cataloging-in-Publication Data
Coile, D. Caroline.
    Pekingese : everything about adoption, purchase, care, nutrition, behavior, and training / D. Caroline Coile ; illustrations by Michele Earle-Bridges.
        p.   cm.—(A complete pet owner's manual)
    Includes bibliographical references and index.
    ISBN 0-8120-9676-2
    1. Pekingese dog. I. Earle-Bridges, Michele.
II. Title. III. Series.
SF429.P3C58   1996
    636.7'6—dc20   96-1967
                                                          CIP

Printed in China

19 18 17 16 15 14 13 12

Acknowledgments

The information contained in this book comes from a variety of sources: breeders, original research, scientific articles, veterinary journals, and a library of dog books. But by far my most heartfelt gratitude must go to my most demanding teachers, who have taught me the skills of both home repair and dog repair, allowed ample testing opportunities for behavioral problem cures, and whetted my curiosity (and carpets) about everything canine for the past 20 years: Baha, Khyber, Tundra, Kara, Hypatia, Savannah, Sissy, Dixie, Bobby, Kitty, Jeepers, Bean-Boy, Junior, Khyzi, Wolfman, Stinky, Honey, and Luna.

Photo Credits

Bob Schwartz: front cover, inside front cover, inside back cover, pages 8, 32 bottom, 41, 64 bottom, 65, 76; Wendy & Richard Moore: back cover; Steve Bonet: page 17 bottom; Paulette Braun: pages 9 top, 16, 21, 24, 32 top; Marilyn LaBrache Brown: pages 5, 64 top, 84; D. Caroline Coile: page 92; Lainie Jones: page 9 bottom left; Bonnie Nance: pages 13 top, 20, 29, 33, 36, 37, 45, 52, 56, 57, 61, 73, 89, 93; Richard Albee: pages 17 top, 81; Nancy Ross: pages 60, 68, 85; Judith Strom: pages 12 bottom, 48, 53; Janet Tucker: page 4; Toni Tucker: pages 12 top, 13 bottom, 25, 28, 72, 88; R. Wood: page 9 bottom right.

Important Note

This pet owner's guide tells the reader how to buy and care for a Pekingese. The author and the publisher consider it important to point out that the advice given in the book is meant primarily for normally developed puppies from a good breeder—that is, dogs of excellent physical health and good character.

Anyone who adopts a fully grown dog should be aware that the animal has already formed its basic impressions of human beings. The new owner should watch the animal carefully, including its behavior toward humans, and should meet the previous owner. If the dog comes from a shelter, it may be possible to get some information on the dog's background and peculiarities there. There are dogs that, as a result of bad experiences with humans, behave in an unnatural manner or may even bite. Only people that have experience with dogs should take in such animals.

Caution is further advised in the association of children with dogs, in meeting with other dogs, and in exercising the dog without a leash.

Even well-behaved and carefully supervised dogs sometimes do damage to someone else's property or cause accidents. It is therefore in the owner's interest to be adequately insured against such eventualities, and we strongly urge all dog owners to purchase a liability policy that covers their dog.

Contents

The Pekingese—living treasure of the Orient.

Preface

The Pekingese is a dog like no other.

Pampered by royalty, coveted by the elite, no breed of dog has been the subject of such unabashed adulation for so many centuries. Today the tradition of Pekingese worship continues in homes around the world.

Admirers of the Pekingese are legion, and arguably the most loyal and ardent fanciers of any breed. To own a Pekingese is to fall completely under its spell.

Detractors of the Pekingese abound as well, denouncing the dogs as wimpy, useless lapdogs. These detractors have one thing in common: they obviously do not know the Pekingese!

A wolf in sheep's clothing, the enigmatic Pekingese (Peke to its friends) is a dog full of surprises. This is your invitation to discover this oriental treasure and the secrets it holds so closely, to decide if you are fit to share your life with this most unusual of breeds, and to consider the unique health care and grooming needs these little big dogs require.

Serene yet feisty, sedate yet exuberant, haughtily snobbish yet coquettishly playful, highly intelligent yet exasperatingly stubborn, the typical Pekingese almost defies description. One thing is for sure: it is, indeed, a dog like no other. It would never stand for it.

D. Caroline Coile, Ph.D.

A Peek into the Past

Gaze into the eyes of the Pekingese and gaze into the distant past, into a mystical world of emperors and dragons, of symbolism and ceremony. Because the Pekingese is a living artifact, an unbroken genetic link with the ancient imperial world of the Orient. Its ancestors were royalty in every sense of the word—and the Pekingese is not about to let you forget it.

Of Buddha, Lions, and Dogs

The story begins long ago in the Far East. In classical times, China traded with Tibet, Rome, and Egypt, and Maltese dogs from Rome were probably introduced to Tibet and China by way of these traders. The dogs of ancient China included hunting dogs, watch dogs, and larder dogs of the chow chow type, but there were also small, puglike dogs with short muzzles known as "ha pa" ("under table") dogs, which appear to have been kept as pets by the wealthier people as early as 700 B.C. The ha pa, possibly with influence from the Maltese, is probably the foundation of the "lion dog," the earliest incarnation of the Pekingese.

The Pekingese owes its most revered existence to the spread of the Lamaist form of Buddhism to China from Tibet around 700 A.D. One of the strongest Lamaist symbols of Buddha was the lion, a wild beast tamed by Buddha to become his faithful servant. The lion of Buddha could appear in different-sized forms; in fact, one charming and often cited legend tells of how the lion implored Buddha to make it smaller, but to retain its great heart, so that it might court the mar-moset it loved so much. Buddha granted the lion's wish, in so doing creating the diminutive lion dog with the size of the marmoset and the great heart and courage of the lion.

Because there were no lions in China, the Foo dogs of the palace (probably a derivative of the ha pa dog), which bore a remarkable resemblance to a tiny lion, soon replaced the lion as the exalted symbol of Buddha. The Chinese were masters at creating beauty and art in a variety of ways, including shaping living plants and animals to comply with their sense of aesthetics. The lion dog was perhaps their crowning glory.

Much of the success of the Chinese in breeding these fabulous little lions lay in the unlimited resources available to the emperors who directed their

Weighing as little as four pounds, the tiny sleeve Pekes have always found special favor.

The Pekingese is a living work of art; a true treasure from the Orient.

production. Palace eunuchs were in charge of extensive breeding operations. The Tibetan monks also had the resources and time to devote to breeding dogs, and they, too, developed a small temple dog that may have been incorporated into the development of the Chinese lion dog.

Life in the Palace

The emperors of the T'ang dynasty (700 A.D. to 1000 A.D.) were especially devoted to the lion dogs and their mystical connotations, and it was during this era that the lion dog was perfected, and emerged as a unique breed. As the living symbol of Buddha, the lion dogs of the palace lived lives of splendor and luxury. At the height of their favor they were literally treated as royalty, some even being given royal appointments. The finest dogs were guarded and pampered by their per-

sonal servants, fed the choicest foods, and bathed in perfumes. The smallest dogs found special favor as "sleeve dogs," and were carried about in the huge sleeves of the robes worn by both men and women. Pekingese partook in all ceremonial affairs, bedecked with ribbons and bells, some preceding the emperor and announcing his arrival with short barks, while others trailed behind to carry the train of the emperor's robe. The penalty for taking such an exalted animal from the palace was "death by a thousand cuts." Yet such were the rewards for smuggling that the eunuchs often arranged for dogs to be spirited away, so that these royal dogs eventually found their way into the homes of wealthy Chinese and even Europeans.

The most popular colors of the dogs within the palace were the fawns and reds, perhaps because they were the most lionlike. However, dogs having a white mark in the center of their forehead were also favored, because this mark was said to be one of Buddha's superior marks. Also in favor was a sashlike mark on the body, suggestive of the yellow sash worn by some members of the imperial family.

Very few breeds can claim so long a period of sustained selective breeding and exaltation as can the lion dog. The lion dog remained an important religious symbol throughout the Han, T'ang, Sung, and Mongul dynasties. Only during the Ming dynasty did the popularity of the lion dog cult wane, accompanied by a decline in Buddhism. Still, the lion dogs remained as pets of the eunuchs and women, albeit without the fanfare once accorded them. And although the eating of dogs was common practice, the lion dogs were never among the breeds included on the menu. When the Ming dynasty was overthrown by the Manchus in the seventeenth century, Buddhism returned to favor and the lion dogs were once again embraced as religious symbols.

Although occasional lion dogs had made their way to Europe, they were not maintained there as a breed, and so had little influence in the western world until the magnificent Summer Palace was looted by British and other troops in 1860. The emperor and his family fled, apparently taking with them many of the nearly 100 dogs normally in the palace, and leaving orders that the remainder be executed rather than fall into foreign hands. But left behind were five lion dogs belonging to the emperor's aunt, who had taken her own life. The dogs were taken to England, where one (a fawn and white, later named "Lootie") was presented to Queen Victoria, and the others were bred. Most of all, these oriental treasures enchanted everyone who saw them.

The Legacy

This was the beginning of the end of imperial China; the last Dowager Empress T'Zu Hsi died in 1908, and was laid to rest amid ceremonies that included models of her favorite lion dog. She left behind a poem describing the lion dog (from which many claim the current official standard was derived) and a legacy of some of the finest dogs the world had ever seen. The lion dog was left in the hands of occidental fanciers, as it all but vanished from its homeland.

The Occidental Tourist

Europe: There were still lion dogs in China, but the large-scale breeding within the palaces would never be seen again. The lion dog had become the pet of the common people, having been made available through the disposition of dogs bred in the palace but not considered of high enough quality to keep. Some of the dogs made available in this way at the monthly trading fairs were probably the source for many of the early importations. Others were forcibly taken from pet owners by the occupying troops. Unfortunately, since these dogs did not represent the imperial ideals, they did not form a good genetic basis for the breed in Europe. However, an occasional palace dog was allowed to leave for Europe. Two such dogs were "Ah Cum" and "Mimosa" in 1896, who, along with "Boxer," can be found heading many modern-day pedigrees.

The first Pekingese sauntered into an English show ring in 1893, and the first was registered in 1898, amid continuing disagreement over what to call this breed. The Chinese had never referred to it as a "Pekingese," but the Europeans had naturally dubbed it after the city in which it had been discovered. The next decade saw the formation of several breed clubs with different ideas over the proper name as well as type and size, but "Pekingese" finally became the officially and commonly recognized name for the lion dog.

America: The Pekingese was meanwhile arriving in America, often a treasured souvenir of the trips abroad made by the affluent. In 1906, the American Kennel Club officially recognized the Pekingese. The early specialty shows held by the Pekingese Club of America were fabulous social events, attracting not only hundreds of Pekingese, but perhaps the most elite exhibitors ever seen at a dog show. Prices for puppies were spectacularly high and the Pekingese was clearly the breed of high society.

At the Peak

Although these oriental wonders attracted much attention, their small litters kept their numbers down, and many of the breed's early fanciers were not interested in selling their precious stock. The breed could count

Today, the Pekingese is among the most popular of toy breeds, providing a rare opportunity for commoners to mingle with royalty. Yet the Pekingese seems content to put up with having only one person to take the place of its multitude of servants, guards, and admirers of the past; in fact, as long as it is treated royally, it will deign to accept its family as royalty as well.

No breed of dog has been held in such high esteem for so long a period of time as has the Pekingese. As you get to know this breed, perhaps you will understand why, and perhaps you, too, will become one of its many worshippers. Because the cult of the lion dog is still going strong.

Peeking into the Future

Thousands of generations of selective breeding should produce a dog that is consistently near perfection. Unfortunately, as the Pekingese became more popular, opportunists saw the chance to cash in by breeding and selling puppies, and naive pet owners bred their beloved but often poor quality Pekingese without understanding the harm they were doing. With each such careless breeding, the centuries of utter devotion to perfecting the lion dog were negated. While there remain breeders who are every bit as dedicated to preserving and perfecting the lion dog as were the emperors of the past, they must constantly fight against the tide of puppies produced by those who do not know, or do not care. The majestic lion dog, symbol of Buddha, living antique, faces its greatest challenge ever from those who would claim to love it without bothering to understand it.

The Pekingese—a prize to be treasured.

as its devotees some of the West's most influential businessmen, politicians, and royalty. When the breed finally became available to everyday pet owners and dog fanciers, it began a meteoric rise to the top.

With a commanding presence, the Pekingese is among the most regal of dogs.

The Pekingese is still casting its spell upon those who get to know it.

With its mysterious past and majestic dwarf-lion appearance, the Pekingese quickly became among the most coveted of Oriental imports.

Peke Perks and Pitfalls

No animal species has proven to be more malleable in human hands than has the dog. Selectively bred to serve people in a multitude of roles, dogs range in size and shape more than any other species, with a comparable range in behavior. To the uninitiated, all dogs act alike. But in fact, the very basis of selection for different tasks was the propensity of different dogs to act in different ways, and scientific studies have demonstrated time and again that there are, indeed, striking hereditary differences in behavior among breeds of dogs. The Pekingese is a product of thousands of generations of selective breeding for imperial demeanor as well as lionlike appearance and beauty. It does not look like other breeds, and it does not act like other breeds, nor should it be expected to.

The Pekingese Personality

The Pekingese still plays the role of royal dog with the same calm dignity that it must have displayed in the emperor's palace. As befitting an object of adulation, the Pekingese is gentle but condescending, and remains aloof with strangers. This is the public Pekingese—haughty, deliberate, regal, and sedate. But the private Pekingese is another animal entirely. How the women and children must have delighted in the behind-the-scenes antics of these little lion clowns, because around its family, the Pekingese is apt to change from court royalty to court jester, uncovering a joie de vivre and remarkable sense of humor reserved to share only with a special few.

The Wild Side

The Pekingese has a few more surprises in store for those who get to know it. First of all, contrary to popular belief, this is no "sissy" lapdog. Even extensive selection for royal demeanor could not erase the natural instinct of the Pekingese to, at times, just be a dog. The Peke likes nothing better than a jaunt afield, where it will give chase to a rabbit with a fervor that would make any beagle blush. It also will not hesitate to plunge into a lake, poke its flat face deep into a hole, or subject its magnificent coat to an occasional mudpack and cocklebur beauty treatment. This stately palace dog has a definite wild side.

In fact, the Pekingese is a tough character. It will not start a fracas, but it will never back down from one. Its courage is virtually boundless. This courageous attitude, coupled with its calm disposition, makes the Pekingese the ideal watchdog. It does not yap incessantly, or call the alarm to a falling leaf, but when it does bark, its owner can be sure that there is something of which to take note.

Many dogs are dependent upon their owners, looking to them for guidance at every turn. Not so the Pekingese. It is fiercely independent, and this trait, combined with its indisputably strong will, can be exasperating to the first-time Peke owner. The Pekingese does not have a stubborn streak; it has a stubborn body. When the Pekingese plants its feet and says "No," it becomes a canine anchor. Attempts to force it into compliance result in only more determination to have its own way. When it comes to doing nothing, despite all urging to the contrary, the Pekingese is among the unchallenged masters of dogdom.

Pekingese are extremely intelligent dogs but they need intelligent trainers who can mold their training techniques to work with, rather than against, a dog that does not act like most other dogs. Trained correctly, the Pekingese can be an obedient and trustworthy companion; yet it will never be a fawning slave.

As befitting any royalty, the Pekingese does not immediately take to strangers. It is a one-family dog, and does not hesitate to discriminate between family and non-family. Still, with time it will gradually warm up to new acquaintances, and once accepted as friend, it displays undying loyalty and devotion. Indeed, one of the breed's great charms is that it requires people to earn its friendship, unlike so many breeds that seem all too eager to abandon their family for the first stranger that throws a ball.

The Pekingese loves its family dearly, but it is not overly demonstrative. Apart from an exuberant greeting, it prefers to honor its loved ones with an occasional kiss, never indiscriminately nor insincerely given. Not a lapdog by nature, the Pekingese will nonetheless acquiesce to sitting in your lap if you ask it nicely. Although left to its own it would probably prefer to sit very close by your side as an equal, it will trade a slight loss in dignity for a soft caress.

The Pekingese is indeed royalty, and it will never let you forget it. But it is equally willing to appoint its family as royalty as well, and make its home, no matter how humble, an imperial palace.

The Pekingese Physiology

The Pekingese is a brachycephalic, exophthalmic, prognathic, achondroplastic dwarf. And proud of it.

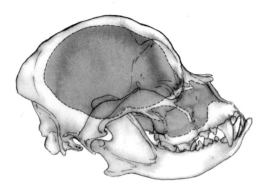

The Pekingese skull. Note the prognathic (undershot) bite and limited nasal area.

Brachycephalic is the term for skulls having a shortened muzzle and flat face. One of the jobs of the nasal passages in a dog is to act as a sort of radiator for the body. The longer the nasal airways (as well as tongue), the better the cooling that the dog can achieve by panting. Many brachycephalic breeds also have a tendency to have elongated palates, which can swell and partially obstruct breathing if the dog pants excessively. Overheating is a major life-threatening condition of the Pekingese.

Exophthalmic describes the Peke's prominent, sometimes bulging eyes. The prominence of the eyes renders them susceptible to injury and the Peke owner must be ever alert for eye abrasions that could result in serious discomfort or blindness. The eyes of carefully bred Pekes protrude less than do those of poorly bred pet-quality Pekes, and in general, today's well-bred Peke has far fewer eye problems than in the past.

Prognathicism is the term for an underbite, where the bottom teeth protrude farther forward than the top teeth. Undesirable in most breeds, it is the proper and typical jaw conformation for the Pekingese—within limits.

If the eyes are the windows to the soul, then the Pekingese has the best views in all dogdom!

legs. Achondroplastic dwarf breeds tend to have a characteristic bow to their front legs, so that the leg turns in around the pasterns but back out again around the feet. This conformation results in the Pekingese characteristic rolling gait, and also renders it an unlikely Olympic hopeful.

Purebreds, Pekingese, and Predispositions

Purebred dog breeders are sometimes accused of breeding with no regard to health in quest of exaggerated dogs capable of bringing home show awards. No reputable breeder is oblivious to health problems. However, as a breed becomes more popular, more people are tempted to breed "just one litter," and usually do so with no information about health problems or about the health of dogs in their dog's background. In addition, "puppy mills" breed dogs with no regard for health attributes, resulting in a genetic disaster for the breed. Who gets the blame? The responsible breeder who checks stock for hereditary problems, neuters those who may pass on problems, and gives health guarantees for pups. The backyard breeders and puppy millers continue on, oblivious to the problem they have helped to create, leaving the dedicated breeders holding the bag and picking up the pieces.

Some physical features desired in a breed may inadvertently cause a related health problem. Thus, in the Pekingese, the desired flat face causes problems in breathing and heat dissipation; the prominent eye renders the cornea more subject to injury and drying; and the desired over-nose wrinkle can hold moisture and become inflamed and/or infected. The prevalence of a particular problem may also be because a prominent dog in the founding of the breed happened to carry that fault, and passed it on to most of the breed.

Overdone, the tongue may hang out, and chewing may be difficult.

Achondroplastic dwarf refers to a type of dwarfism caused by arrested development of the long bones, without a concomitant reduction in bone diameter. In a sense, the Pekingese is a rather large, heavy dog with short

The Pekingese can be a fearless character, and will not hesitate to tackle any challenge or engage in boisterous play—as long as it does so in private!

12

The Pekingese has been a popular breed, bred by backyard breeders and puppy millers for a long time. It is also a breed of exaggeration. Besides a predisposition for corneal abrasions and facial wrinkle skin infections, the following problems are also seen with a slightly higher frequency than in most other breeds.

Visual
• Trichiasis (eyelashes that grow in toward the eye, irritating the cornea)
• Distichiasis (an extra row of eyelashes that tend to grow inward and irritate the eye)
• Lacrimal duct atresia (absence of tear duct openings)
• Microphthalmia (abnormally small eye resulting in blindness)
• Juvenile cataract (opacity of the lens at an early age)
• Atypical pannus (progressive opacity of the cornea)
• Progressive retinal atrophy (degeneration of the retina)

Skeletal
• Legg-Calve-Perthes disease (degeneration of the head of the femur [thigh] bone, resulting in pain and hind leg lameness)
• Patellar luxation (dislocation of the kneecap)
• Hypoplasia of dens (underdevelopment of the axis vertebra of the neck), resulting in spinal cord compression
• Intervertebral disc degeneration (protrusion of discs between vertebrae resulting in pain, incoordination, and even paralysis)
• Elbow luxation (improper articulation of the elbow joint)
• Short skull

Other
• Hydrocephalus (excessive accumulation of cerebrospinal fluid in the brain)
• Epilepsy
• Umbilical hernia

The Pekingese expects to be treated as a real family member, and will repay proper treatment with unsurpassed loyalty.

Carefully bred Pekes are relatively free of health problems, and make the best pets because they have the promise of longer, healthier, lives.

• Inguinal hernia (protrusion of abdominal contents through inguinal canal) in the inner thigh
• Cleft palate (incomplete closure of the bony roof of the mouth)
• Elongated soft palate
• Urolith formation tendency (stone formation within the urinary system)
• "Swimmers" (young puppies having flattened bodies and an inability to stand)

Do not be dismayed by what may appear to be a daunting list of disorders. *The typical well-bred Pekingese is healthy and free of any serious genetic problem.* It is the typical poorly bred Pekingese that may not be free of genetic defect, for the simple reason that they are bred by people who are often blissfully ignorant of any problems at all. Even more so than in most breeds, it is essential to carefully select your future Pekingese from a reputable breeder (see Seeking a Peking Dog, beginning on page 19).

Back to Reality

It may be dawning upon you that finding and caring for a Pekingese is going to involve a lot of work. Now is the time to take a step backward and carefully consider what you are doing. A dog is not a trial-run item. It is a sentient being that will not understand why it is being uprooted from its home or banished to the backyard or garage. It will not understand that its family members welcomed it into their home on a whim and then tired of it as they would another toy, or that its coat became so unkempt that it was no longer a pleasure to pet or show off to friends. When you invite a dog into your family, invite it as a real family member, not a passing fancy or a conversation piece.

Count on having your Pekingese for another 12 or so years, on spending a lot of money on veterinary bills, on spending every day feeding, walking, and cleaning up after your dog, and on making sacrifices, whether it be chewed shoes, soiled carpets, or compromised vacations. And count on your dog slowing down and not being quite so playful and entertaining as it grows older.

Besides the daily care that you must give any dog, you must make a commitment to wash and dry your Peke's face and wrinkle daily. You must also commit to (at least) weekly grooming to keep the coat mat-free, and to daily inspection of the coat around the anus to ensure that it has not become soiled.

Hot, or even warm, weather can be deadly to a Pekingese. You must have properly cooled facilities for your prospective Peke. And you must be able to make the financial commitment to run the air-conditioner, if need be, day and night for your dog, even though you may not be at home enjoying it. If you live in a warm climate and cannot make this commitment, in fairness to you and your dog, choose another breed.

Don't expect the children to keep up this burden of care. Some people reason that a dog is a good way to teach children responsibility, but it is not fair to the dog to use its missed dinner as a lesson for Junior. Nor is the Pekingese the appropriate breed for most children. The Peke's somewhat reserved disposition and lack of athletic ability may prove frustrating for some youngsters. Young Peke owners must be gentle and careful around these small dogs.

The Peke of Perfection

The Pekingese was developed through generations of purposeful selective breeding in an attempt to create a little lionlike imperial dog. Today's breeders are guided by an exacting standard of perfection. No one dog ever fits that standard perfectly, but at the very least, a Pekingese should fit the standard well enough so that it is easily recognized as a Pekingese. This possession of breed attributes is known as *type*, and is an important requirement of any purebred. A Pekingese should also be built in such a way that it can go about its daily life with minimal exertion and absence of lameness. This equally important attribute is known as *soundness*. Add to these the attributes of *good health* and *temperament*, and you have the four cornerstones of the ideal Pekingese.

Points of the Pekingese

Like many standards, that of the Pekingese has been rewritten on occasion in order to clarify ambiguous points or emphasize certain important areas. The latest revision of the Pekingese standard was approved in 1995, and is reprinted here.

The 1995 AKC Standard

General Appearance

The Pekingese is a well-balanced, compact dog with heavy front and lighter hindquarters. It must suggest its Chinese origin in its directness, independence, individuality and expression. Its image is lionlike. It should imply courage, boldness, and self-esteem rather than prettiness, daintiness, or delicacy.

Size, Substance, Proportion

Size/Substance: The Pekingese should be surprisingly heavy when lifted. It has a stocky, muscular body. The bone of the forequarters must be very heavy in relation to the size of the dog. All weights are correct within the limit of 14 pounds (6.4 kg), provided that type and points are not sacrificed.

Disqualification: Weight over 14 pounds (6.4 kg).

Proportion: The length of the body, from the front to the breastbone in a straight line to the buttocks, is slightly

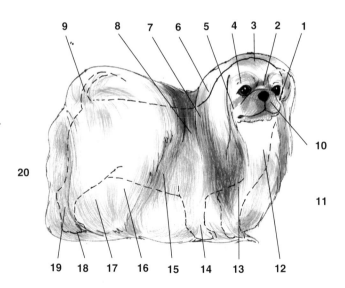

Parts of the Pekingese. 1. Muzzle, 2. stop, 3. skull, 4. eye, 5. cheek, 6. ear, 7. withers, 8. shoulder, 9. tail, 10. nose, 11. forequarters, 12. brisket, 13. chest, 14. pastern, 15. ribcage, 16. loin, 17. stifle, 18. metatarsal, 19. hock, 20. hindquarters

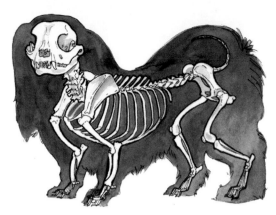

The Pekingese skeleton. As an achondroplastic dwarf, the front legs are supposed to be bowed outward.

greater than the height at the withers. Overall balance is of utmost importance.

Head

Skull: The topskull is massive, broad, and flat (not dome-shaped). The topskull, the high, wide cheekbones, broad lower jaw, and wide chin are the structural formation of the correctly shaped face. When viewed frontally, the skull is wider than deep and contributes to the rectangular envelope-shaped appearance of the head. In profile, the Pekingese face

The correct Pekingese is lionlike and compactly built, heavier in the front than in the rear, and with an expression of Oriental dignity.

must be flat. The chin, nose leather, and brow all lie in one plane. In the natural position of the head, this plane appears vertical but slants very slightly backward from forehead to chin.

Nose: It is black, broad, very short, and in profile, contributes to the flat appearance of the face. Nostrils are open. The nose is positioned between the eyes so that a line drawn horizontally across the top of the nose intersects the center of the eyes.

Eyes: They are large, very dark, round, lustrous, and set wide apart. The look is bold, not bulging. The eye rims are black and the white of the eye does not show when the dog is looking straight ahead.

Wrinkle: It effectively separates the upper and lower areas of the face. The appearance is of a hair-covered fold of skin, extending from one cheek, over the bridge of the nose in a wide inverted "V," to the other cheek. It is NEVER so prominent or heavy as to crowd the facial features nor to obscure a large portion of the eyes or the nose from view.

Stop: It is deep. The bridge of the nose is completely obscured from view by hair and/or the over-nose wrinkle.

Muzzle: This is very short and broad with high, wide cheek bones. The color of the skin is black. Whiskers add to the oriental expression.

Mouth: The lower jaw is slightly undershot. The lips meet on a level plane and neither teeth nor tongue show when the mouth is closed. The lower jaw is strong, wide, firm and straight across at the chin. An excessively strong chin is as undesirable as a weak one.

Ears: They are heart-shaped and set on the front corners of the skull extending the line of the topskull. Correctly placed ears frame the sides of the face and with their heavy feathering create an illusion of additional width of the head.

Pigment: The skin of the nose, lips, and eye rims is black on all colors.

Neck, Body, Tail
Neck: It is very short, thick, and set back into the shoulder.
Body: This is pear-shaped and compact. It is heavy in front with well-sprung ribs slung between the forelegs. The broad chest, with little or no protruding breastbone, tapers to lighter loins with a distinct waist. The topline is level.
Tail: The base is set high; the remainder is carried well over the center of the back. Long, profuse straight feathering may fall to either side.

Forequarters
They are short, thick, and heavy-boned. The bones of the forelegs are slightly bowed between the pastern and elbow. Shoulders are gently laid back and fit smoothly into the body. The elbows are always close to the body. Front feet are large, flat, and turned slightly out. The dog must stand well up on feet.

Hindquarters
They are lighter in bone than the forequarters. There is moderate angulation and definition of stifle and hock. When viewed from behind, the rear legs are reasonably close and parallel and the feet point straight ahead.
Soundness is essential in both forequarters and hindquarters.

Coat
Body Coat: It is full-bodied, with long, coarse-textured, straight, stand-off coat, and thick, softer undercoat. The coat forms a noticeable mane on the neck and shoulder area with the coat on the remainder of the body somewhat shorter in length. A long and profuse coat is desirable providing it does not obscure the shapeliness of the body, nor sacrifice the correct coat texture.

The crowning glory of royalty, the Peke's coat should form a lionlike mane around the neck and shoulders.

Feathering: Long feathering is found on the back of the thighs and forelegs, and on the ears, tail, and toes. The feathering is left on the toes but should not be so long as to prevent free movement.

The massive skull with broad flat face and high positioned nose is an integral facet of Pekingese type.

Color

All coat colors and markings, including parti-colors, are allowable and of equal merit.

Gait

The gait is unhurried and dignified, with a slight roll over the shoulders. The rolling gait is caused by the bowed front legs and heavier, wider forequarters pivoting on the tapered waist and the lighter, straight parallel hindquarters. The rolling motion is smooth and effortless and is as free as possible from bouncing, prancing, or jarring.

Temperament

A combination of regal dignity, self-importance, self-confidence and exasperating stubbornness make for a good-natured, lively, and affectionate companion to those who have earned its respect.

The foregoing is a description of the ideal Pekingese. Any deviation should be penalized in direct proportion to the extent of that deviation.

Faults to Be Noted

- Dudley, liver, or gray nose
- Light brown, yellow, or blue eyes
- Protruding tongue or teeth
- Overshot upper jaw
- Wry mouth
- Ears set much too high, low, or far back
- Roach or swayback
- Straight-boned forelegs

	Points:
Expression	5
Nose	5
Stop	5
Muzzle	5
Legs and Feet	15
Tail	5
Skull	10
Eyes	5
Ears	5
Shape of Body	20
Coat, feather, and condition	10
Action	10
Total	100

Disqualification—weight over 14 pounds.

Terminology

- Angulation: Angle formed by the shoulder blade and upper arm in the forequarters, and the pelvis, stifle, and hock in the rear quarters
- Dudley nose: Flesh-colored nose
- Overshot front teeth: Incisors of the top jaw projecting beyond those of the bottom jaw
- Stop: Transition area from forehead to muzzle
- Topskull: Top of the head, between the ears

Seeking a Peking Dog

Your Pekingese can be purchased either directly from a breeder or from a pet store. A pet store should be able to provide the same information about a puppy's background that you would get directly from a breeder, such as the pedigrees and health records of the puppy's parents; whether the puppy was raised around people or in a cage; how long it stayed with the mother; and so forth. The store should also guarantee that it will take back the puppy if it becomes ill. Your Pekingese should come from a source that appreciates and nurtures the special heritage and character of this breed. Your Peke will be a part of your family and life for the next 10 to 15 years. Spend the time now to make those years the best possible.

Buyer Beware

Many people mistakenly believe that the phrase "AKC registered" is an assurance of quality. But it can no more assure quality than the registration of your car is an assurance of automotive quality. Few people would buy a car from a stranger without extensive checking and testing, but many people buy the first Peke they find based only upon the fact that it is AKC registered.

Whether you want pet, show, or breeding quality you must be very careful about where you find your Pekingese. You want to avoid a puppy from parents whose only claim to breeding quality is fertility. And you want to avoid buying from a breeder whose only claim to that title is owning a fertile Pekingese. You may think that if you only want pet quality you don't have to be so careful. But consider the most important attributes of a pet: good health and good temperament.

Buy the best dog, with the best par-

ents, from the best breeder possible. The optimum situation would be if you could actually see the parents and puppies, and if you get some type of guarantee. A word of caution about guarantees from any source: No guarantee can reimburse you for your broken heart when your puppy dies. And replacement guarantees that require you to return the original dog aren't worth much when you already love that original dog.

Pet, Show, or Breeding Quality?

One of the reasons for choosing a purebred dog is the assurance that it will look and act a certain way when it

Pekingese come in many colors and types. The tiny sleeve Peke (rear) may be half the size of larger Pekes. They may be of either show or pet quality. The show-quality Peke (middle) embodies the imperial essence of the breed. The pet-quality Peke (front) has the same wonderful temperament, but usually lacks the magnificent coat and other breed features.

Pet-quality Pekes may not have the abundant coat, short legs, or massive head of their show counterparts, but still make delightful lifetime partners.

pet quality not even pet quality: flaws in temperament such as shyness or aggressiveness, or health problems.

Show-quality dogs should first of all be pet quality; that is, they should have good temperament and health. On top of this, they should be able to compete in the show ring with a reasonable expectation of finishing a championship. Your search for a show-quality dog will require you to first study the breed so you can make an educated choice. This is done by talking to breeders and reading about and seeing as many Pekes as possible.

With few exceptions, breeding-quality dogs come from impeccable backgrounds, and are of even higher show quality than are show-quality dogs. The very small "sleeve" females are too small to breed safely. It is difficult to pick a show-quality puppy at an early age; it is impossible to pick a breeding-quality puppy.

Sources of Pekingese

Breed clubs and rescue organizations: The Pekingese Club of America is an excellent source of reputable breeders. In addition, if you are interested in an older dog, ask to be put in contact with the breed rescue group, which finds homes for Pekes in distress.

Animal shelters: To see this royal dog in an animal shelter, still maintaining its pride despite the indignities it has suffered, is a vision not easily forgotten. As much as you may be tempted to rush in and save one of these souls, take the time to first ascertain why that particular Peke did not work out for its former owner. Although adopting a dog often means a lot of work, there is immense satisfaction in knowing that you are that dog's savior, and that you are offering it a life filled with love, nurturing, and understanding that it may never have experienced before, but always deserved.

matures. In many breeds the differences in quality are only apparent to fanciers of that breed. The Pekingese is not one of them. Unfortunately, all Pekingese are not created equal.

Dogs can be graded as pet, show, and breeding quality. Pet-quality dogs have one or more traits that would make winning with them in the show ring difficult to impossible, such as the failure of one or both testicles to descend into the scrotum, an improper bite, straight front legs, or a poor tail set. All make beautiful pets. More severe flaws are those that make a Peke non-Pekelike, such as long legs, short coat, overly large size, or pointed face. Finally, there are flaws that make

Pet shops: A pet shop should be able to provide the same information about a puppy's background that you would get directly from the breeder. Ask if you can contact the breeder or be provided with information from the breeder about the pedigrees of the puppy's parents; whether the puppy was raised around people or in a cage; how long it stayed with the mother; and so forth. It would be ideal if you could visit the breeder or see photos of the breeder's facilities and the puppy with its siblings and mother. Finally, because the Pekingese has special health needs, it is important that you obtain information about the health of the puppy's parents and a guarantee that the shop will take back the puppy if it becomes ill.

Newspaper advertisements: Most newspaper ads are placed by backyard breeders who know nothing about breeding quality puppies. There are exceptions, however, so that if the ad is worded in a knowledgeable and responsible way, it could be that the breeder is reputable. An ad that mentions titled parents, home-raised pups, health guarantee, and availability of breed information, might be worth checking. Stay away from ads that use the terms *thoroughbreds*, or *full-blooded*, or *papered*, all of which are not terms a knowledgeable breeder would use. Don't be impressed by the promise of "champion pedigree." In virtually any pedigree you will find many champions, and if these champions are more than two generations back, their impact upon these puppies is minimal. Nor should you be impressed by the statement that the pups have been vaccinated and wormed. All puppies should be vaccinated and wormed by selling age, so if the breeder considers this a big deal, these pups probably don't have a lot going for them.

Dog magazines: Serious breeders can be found through one of the all-breed dog magazines available at

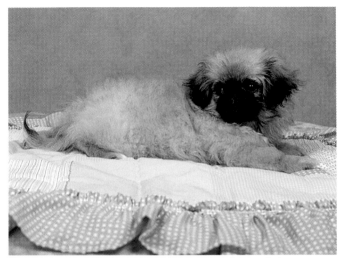

A puppy requires the same watchful care as a human baby.

larger newsstands. Even better is the current issue of the *Orient Express* (see address on page 94). The disadvantage is that if the breeder is located some distance from you, you will not be able to evaluate the dogs in the flesh, and you will not be able to choose your own puppy. Also, shipping adds an additional expense and can be more stressful for an older puppy.

Dog shows: If at all possible attend a dog show. You can contact the AKC for the date of a show in your area; these are also listed in *Dog World* magazine (see address on page 94). Most shows start at 8:00 A.M., so unless you know when the Pekingese are being judged, you must get there early or risk missing them altogether. Tell the Pekingese exhibitors of your interest and arrange to talk with several after they have finished in the show ring.

Why a Show Breeder?

Why contact a show breeder if all you want is a pet? Because these breeders will have raised your pet as

21

though it were their next Best in Show winner. It will have received the same prenatal care, nutrition, and socialization as every prospective show dog in that litter. And the breeder should be knowledgeable and conscientious enough to have also considered temperament and health when planning the breeding. If this is to be your first Pekingese, you will need continued advice from an experienced Peke owner as your puppy grows. The serious hobby breeder is just a phone call away, and will be concerned that both you and the puppy are getting along well. In fact, because many breeders will expect to keep in touch with the owners of all of the puppies, whether pet or show, throughout their lives, you may find yourself a member of an adopted extended family of sorts, all of whom are available for advice, help, consolation, and celebration.

Questions, Questions

When you contact breeders, tell them exactly what qualities you want in a Peke, if you have a sex, color, or age preference, and whether you want pet or show quality. A good breeder should in turn ask you about your previous experience with dogs, why you want a Pekingese, and what living arrangements you have planned for the dog.

Ask about the parents. Do they have conformation or obedience titles? This is not only important if you want a show/obedience prospect, but again can give you a clue about the care taken with the litter. What kind of temperaments do the parents and the puppies have? Have the parents or puppies had any health problems? Why did they breed the litter? How did they choose the sire?

Papers

Ask about the terms of sale. Don't fall in love with a puppy and then have to walk away because an agreement

could not be reached. There are several possibilities, the easiest being that you will pay a set amount (usually cash) and receive full ownership. Registration papers should not cost extra. Sometimes breeders will insist upon having a pet puppy neutered before supplying the papers, or they may stipulate that a pet puppy is to have a "Limited Registration," which means it cannot be shown or bred. These arrangements are acceptable but should be in writing. If you are making installment payments, the breeder will probably retain the papers or a co-ownership until the last installment. Sometimes a breeder will insist upon co-owning the puppy permanently. Avoid agreements that involve future breeding of the puppy (especially a female) and "puppy-back" agreements. If the co-ownership is for insurance that the dog will be returned to the breeder in the event you cannot keep it, then such an agreement is usually acceptable. Any such terms should be in writing.

Cost

Pekingese are relatively expensive dogs. This in part simply reflects the fact that they are expensive to produce. Caesarean sections are often needed, and litters are very small. Expect to pay $500 for a good pet-quality Pekingese from a good, healthy background, and $1,000 or up for a show-quality Peke. The tiny sleeve Pekes will often be even more costly. Don't expect any good breeder to sell a newcomer a true breeding-quality Peke at any (reasonable) price.

In Search of the Perfect Pekingese

After deciding on your source, take the time to consider Pekingese preferences. Besides color and size, the most common dilemmas concern age and sex.

Puppy or adult? Although most prospective owners think in terms of getting a puppy, don't dismiss the idea of acquiring an older Peke. No one can deny that a puppy is cute and fun, but a puppy is much like a baby—you can't ever be too busy to walk, feed, supervise, or clean it. If you work or have limited patience, consider an older puppy or adult, which won't require so much intensive care.

Ideally, most puppies are brought home between 8 and 12 weeks of age, but if you definitely want a show-quality dog, you may have to wait until the pups are much older, probably five to six months of age. No matter what the age, if the puppy has been properly socialized, it will soon blend into your family life and love you as though it's always owned you.

Pekingese hes and shes. The choice of male versus female is largely one of personal preference. Both have comparably wonderful personalities, but keep the following pros and cons in mind.

Females are slightly smaller, with less profuse coat, than males. They come in estrus ("season" or "heat") twice a year; this lasts for three weeks, during which time you must keep her away from amorous neighborhood males who have chosen your house as the place to be. You must also contend with her bloody discharge during her season. Males, on the other hand, are apt to mark the inside of your house if the mood strikes them, lifting a leg on your white sofa or draperies.

Most of the problems associated with either sex can be overcome by neutering. Spaying before the first season greatly reduces the chances of breast or uterine cancer, and castration lessens the chance of testicular or prostate cancer.

Color choices. Pekingese come in a wide array of colors, but most people

Pay careful attention to the breeder's instructions. During your initial visit, both you and the breeder will be evaluating one another.

think only of the familiar black-masked fawn. True, this color does seem to highlight the Peke's oriental expression, but the angelic pure whites, enchanting soft creams, striking pitch blacks, and captivating parti-colors are all beautiful alternatives if you want something a little out of the ordinary.

How to Pick a Peke

Once you have narrowed down your list, try to visit the breeder. Most modern "kennels" are a collection of only a few dogs that are first of all the breeder's pets. However large or small the operation, look for facilities that are clean and safe. Again, these are clues about the care given your prospective puppy:

• Although it is virtually impossible to keep a litter of puppies from creating an ongoing catastrophe, any messes should be obviously new. Old droppings are a sign of poor hygiene, and poor hygiene is a precursor to poor health.

• The adults should be clean, groomed, and in apparent good health. Note that many owners clip down their

As appealing an idea as it may seem, fight the urge to give a dog for Christmas, or as any surprise gift.

Handling the Puppies

These puppies are fragile little beings, and you must be extremely careful where you step and how you handle them. If you have children with you, don't allow them to run around or play with the puppies unsupervised. In fact, a responsible breeder will send you away puppyless if your children can't control themselves suitably during even a short visit. In addition, your entire family should know how to properly hold a puppy. Never pick a puppy up by its legs or head or tail; cradle the puppy with both hands, one under the chest, the other under the hindquarters, and with the side of the pup secure against your chest. Keep a firm hold lest the pup tries to squirm out of your arms unexpectedly. When placing the pup down, make sure all four legs are on the ground before

retired Pekes so that they can lead a more carefree life.

• Adults should neither try to attack you nor cower from you. Look to the adults for the dog your puppy will become. If you don't care for their looks or temperaments, say good-bye.
• Do make allowances for the dam's ordeal of carrying and nursing, especially in the coat department. Ask to see a picture of her in full bloom.

Don't visit from one breeder to another on the same day, and certainly do not visit the animal shelter beforehand. Puppies are vulnerable to many deadly diseases that you can transmit through your hands, clothes, and shoes. How tragic it would be if the breeder's invitation for you to view their darlings ended up killing them!

Always go to view the puppies prepared to leave without one if you don't see exactly what you want. Remember, no good breeder wants you to take a puppy you are not 110 percent crazy about. This is not something you can trade in once you find what you really want. Don't lead the breeder on if you have decided against a purchase; there may be another buyer in line.

Teach children to respect the puppy's feelings, beginning with instruction on how to hold it. Cradle the pup under its chest and rear, and hold it securely next to your own body.

letting go of it. Even at a young age, mistreatment or negligence can damage your puppy's temperament or health, so watch the breeder to see that he or she treats the pups with love and gentleness.

What to Look for in Peke Puppies

As you finally look upon this family of royal tumbleweeds, you may find it very difficult to be objective. How will you ever decide? If you want a show puppy, let the breeder decide. In fact, the breeder knows the puppies' personalities better than you will in the short time you can evaluate them, so listen carefully to any suggestions the breeder has, even for a pet. But first decide if this is the litter for you. Look for the following:
• By eight weeks of age, Peke pups should look like little puff balls with flat faces. Dark nose pigmentation, absent at birth, should be present by this age.
• Normal Peke puppies are friendly, curious, and attentive. If they are apathetic or sleeping, it could be because they have just eaten, but it could also be because they are sickly.
• The puppies should be clean, with no missing hair, crusted or reddened skin, or signs of parasites.
• Eyes, ears, and nose should be free of discharge.
• Look carefully at the eyes. They should not bulge excessively, deviate to either side, or be reddened or crusted.
• Examine the eyelids to ensure that the lids or lashes don't roll in on the eye.
• The teeth should be straight and meet up evenly, with the bottom incisors in front of the top incisors.
• The gums should be pink; pale gums may indicate anemia.
• The area around the anus should have no hint of irritation or recent diarrhea.

• Puppies should not be thin or excessively potbellied. The belly should have no large bumps indicating a hernia.
• By the age of 12 weeks, male puppies should have both testicles descended in the scrotum.

If the puppy of your choice is limping, or exhibits any of the above traits, express your concern and ask to either come back the following week to see if it has improved, or to have your veterinarian examine it. In fact, any puppy you buy should be done so with the stipulation that it is pending a health check (at your expense) by your veterinarian. The breeder should furnish you with a complete medical history including dates of vaccinations and worming.

Pekingese come in a a wide variety of colors, one of the most eye-catching of which is the spell-binding black.

You may still find it nearly impossible to decide which rolling dust bunny will be yours. Don't worry—no matter which one you choose, it will be the best one. In years to come you will wonder how you were so lucky to have picked the perfect Pekingese. You must realize that your Peke will be perfect in part because you are going to make it that way!

Blue Bloods and Blue Slips

You should not leave with your puppy without the blue AKC registration application signed by both you and the breeder. This is an extremely valuable document—do not misplace it or forget to send it in before the time limit. Ask the breeder if there are any requirements concerning the puppy's registered name; most show breeders will want the first name to be their kennel name. You should also have received a pedigree with your puppy; if not, you can buy a copy of its pedigree from the AKC when you send in the registration papers.

Be sure to ask the breeder what words your puppy knows. Your pup will learn a new name quickly, especially if it means food or fun is on the way. Be careful about the name you choose— for example, "Nomad" sounds like both "no" and "bad," and could confuse a dog. Test your chosen name to be sure that it does not sound like a reprimand or command.

A Puppy for Christmas?

If you are contemplating bringing your pup home as a Christmas present, you should think again. The heartwarming scene you may have imagined of the children discovering the puppy asleep on Christmas morning amongst the other gifts beneath the tree is not realistic. The real scene is more often that of a crying, confused puppy who may have vented its anxiety on the other gifts and left you some

additional "gifts" of its own beneath the tree! Don't bring a new puppy into the hectic chaos of Christmas morning. Not only does this add to what is bound to be a very confusing and intimidating transition for your Peke, but a puppy should not be expected to compete with all of the toys and games that children may be receiving. Every pup needs the undivided attention of its new family at this crucial time in its life. Instead, a photograph or videotape of your special Peke pup-to-be, or a stocking of Pekingese paraphernalia, should provide sufficient surprise, and give the whole family time to prepare.

Red Carpet Welcome

The day you choose your puppy is probably not the best day to bring it home. You need time to prepare for your new family addition, so that when your pup does come home you can give it your individual attention.

If you work away from the home, try to bring your new Pekingese home on a weekend so that it won't have to spend its first day alone. At the same time, don't get the pup so used to your constant presence that when you do have to leave the house and go back to work, it will be a drastic change in its new routine.

Spend some time at the breeder's house while the puppy gets acquainted with you, and listen carefully to the breeder's instructions. Arrange for the puppy to have not eaten before leaving with you; this lessens the possibility of carsickness and helps the puppy learn that you will be its new provider when you get to its new home. The ride home with you may be the puppy's first time in a car, and its first time away from the security of its home and former family. If possible, bring a family member with you to hold and comfort the puppy on the ride home. If it is a long ride, bring a cage. Be sure to take plenty of towels in case it gets carsick.

Never let a new puppy roam around the car, where it can cause—and have—accidents.

Arriving Home

When you get home, put the puppy on lead and carry it to the spot you have decided will be its bathroom. Puppies tend to relieve themselves in areas where they can smell that they have used before. This is why it is so critical to never let the pup have an accident indoors; however, if it does, clean and deodorize the spot thoroughly (using a nonammonia-based cleanser) and keep the pup away from that area. Once the puppy relieves itself, let it explore a little and then offer it a small meal. Now is *not* the time for all the neighbors to come visiting. You want your pup to know who its new family members will be, and too many people will only add to the youngster's confusion. Nor is it the time for rough-and-tumble play, which could scare the puppy. Introductions to other family pets might also be better postponed.

Once the puppy has eaten, it will probably have to relieve itself again, so take it back outside. Praise enthusiastically when it eliminates in the right place. When your Peke begins to act sleepy, place it in its cage (see Cage, page 28) so that it knows this is its special place. A stuffed toy, hot water bottle, or ticking clock may help alleviate some of the anxiety of being left alone. Place the cage in your bedroom for this first night so that the puppy can be comforted by your presence. Remember, this is the scariest thing that has ever happened in your puppy's short life; it has been uprooted from the security of a mother, litter-mates, and loving breeder, so you must be comforting and reassuring on this crucial first night.

You should have so much fun introducing your pup to the world that it will make up for all the work you've taken on. For instance, your pup may very likely even have to be taught how to climb stairs. Going up is usually easy, but down can be difficult for a little long-bodied dog. Start at the bottom of the steps and help your pup one step at a time. This will be your model for everything else you teach your pup— one step at a time.

Loyalty to Royalty

You have a lifetime of experiences to share with your new Pekingese. The remainder of your dog's life will be spent under your care and guidance. Both of you will change through the years. Accept that your Pekingese will change as it matures: from the cute, eager-to-please baby, to the cute, mischievous adolescent, then to the self-reliant adult partner, and finally the proud but somewhat frail senior. Be sure that you remember the promise you made to yourself and your future puppy before you made the commitment to share your life: to keep your interest in your dog, and care for it every day of its life with as much love and enthusiasm as you did the first day it arrived at your home. Your life may change dramatically in the years to come—divorce, new baby, new home—for better or worse, your Pekingese will still depend on you and still love you, and you need to remain as loyal to your Peke as your Peke will be to you.

The Pekingese Pet

After finally locating your Peke-to-be, it's only natural to want to bring it home right away. But first channel your excitement and make sure you and your home are prepared to accept royalty.

Pekingese Purchases

It's not really true that "all you add is love" (but you'll need lots of that, too). Your new Peke pup will need a few necessary items to get started, and you can add as many nonessentials as your budget and good sense will allow. The best places to find these items are at large pet stores, dog shows, or discount pet catalogs.

The traditional wicker basket may end up as a pile of sticks until your Peke is an adult.

The Lion's Den

Cage

One of the larger suggested purchases is a cage. Many new dog owners are initially appalled at the idea of putting their pet in a cage as though it were some wild beast. At times, though, even a Peke pup can be a wild beast, and a cage is one way to save your home from ruination and yourself from insanity. A cage can also provide a quiet haven for your dog. Just as you hopefully find peace and security as you sink into your own bed at night, your pup needs a place that it can call its own, a place it can seek out whenever it needs rest and solitude. The cage should be off-limits to children or anyone who aims to pester the dog. Used properly, your Pekingese will come to think of its cage not as a way to keep itself in, but as a way to keep others out! And by taking the pup directly from the cage to the outdoors upon awakening, the cage will be one of the handiest housebreaking aids at your disposal.

Cages can be abused by overuse. The cage is not a storage box for your dog when you're finished playing with it, nor is it a place of punishment. A cage is the canine equivalent of an infant's crib—a place for naptime where you can leave your pup without fear of it hurting itself or your home and belongings. Place the cage in a corner of a quiet room, but not too far from the rest of the family. Put the pup in the cage when it begins to fall asleep, and it will become accustomed to using it as its bed. Be sure to place a soft pad in the bottom of the cage.

"X-Pen"

An exercise pen ("X-pen") is a transportable wire folding "playpen" for dogs, typically about 4 feet × 4 feet (1.22 m × 1.22 m). If you must be gone for hours at a time, X-pens are the perfect answer because the pup can relieve itself on paper in one corner, sleep on a soft bed in the other, and frolic with its toys all over! It's like having a little yard inside your home.

Your new puppy should not have the run of the entire house. Choose an easily Peke-proofed room where you spend a lot of time, preferably one that is close to a door leading outside. Kitchens and dens are usually ideal. When you must leave your dog alone for some time, you may wish to place it in a cage, X-pen, or secure room. Bathrooms have the disadvantage of being so confining and isolated that puppies may become destructive; if you have no alternative, try using a secure baby gate instead of shutting the door. Garages have the disadvantage of also housing many poisonous items, as well as an array of heavy objects that could fall on an inquisitive pup.

Peke-proofing the Palace

Peke-proofing your home has two goals: protecting your home, and protecting your dog. Home destruction is a major reason that dogs are banished to the backyard or given up for adoption. Yet many people encourage destructive behavior by leaving such an irresistible array of alluring but forbidden objects around that the pup never has a chance.

Get down at puppy level and see what enticements and dangers beckon. Be aware of the following:
• Puppies particularly like to chew items that carry your scent. Shoes, eyeglasses, and clothing must be kept out of the pup's reach.
• Leather furniture is the world's biggest rawhide chewy to a puppy;

Pekingese are true "toy" dogs, not only in size, but in their love of playthings.

wicker furniture can provide hours of chewing entertainment. And Pekes love to shower the room with confetti from your books and papers!
• Your carpets can be partially covered with small washable rugs or indoor-outdoor carpeting until your puppy is housebroken. If you use an X-pen, cover the floor beneath it with thick plastic (an old shower curtain works well), and then add towels or

Household Killers
• Leaked antifreeze
• Rodent baits
• Household cleaners
• Toilet fresheners
• Drugs
• Some houseplants (e.g., Caladium, English Holly, daffodils, Hyacinth bulbs, Philodendron, Mistletoe, and Rhododendron)
• Chocolate (especially baker's chocolate)
• Nuts, bolts, pennies
• Pins and needles
• Bones

The Homecoming Kit

- Buckle collar (cat collar for puppies)—for wearing around the house
- Lightweight leash (nylon, web, or leather, never chain!). An adjustable show lead is great for puppies.
- Stainless steel, flat-bottomed food and water bowls. Avoid plastic, which can cause allergic reactions and hold germs.
- Cage—just large enough for an adult to stand up in
- Exercise pen—24 inches to 30 inches (61–76 cm) tall
- Toys—latex squeakies, fleece-type toys, ball, stuffed animals without loose eyes or other easily detached parts, stuffed socks
- Chewbones—the equivalent of a teething ring for babies
- Anti-chew preparations (e.g. "Bitter Apple")
- Baby gate(s)—better than a closed door for placing parts of your home off limits
- Soft brush
- Wide-tooth comb
- Nail clippers
- Dog shampoo
- First aid kit
- Food. Start with the same food the pup is currently eating (ask the breeder).
- Dog bed. Many pet beds are available, but you can also use the bottom of a plastic cage, or any cozy box. But beware—wicker will most likely be chewed to shreds.
- Camera and film—telephoto lens is a necessity!

Snacks and chewies add a little spice to life.

Dogs, like children, love toys they can call their own.

washable rugs for traction and absorbency.
- Puppies love to chew electrical cords in half, and even lick outlets. These can result in severe burns, loss of the jaw and tongue, and death.
- Jumping up on an unstable object could cause it to come crashing down, perhaps crushing the puppy.
- Do not allow the puppy near the edges of high decks, balconies, or staircases.
- Be on the lookout for anything that might injure an eye.
- Doors can be a hidden danger area. Everyone in your family must be made to understand the danger of slamming a door, which could catch a Peke pup and seriously injure it. Use doorstops to ensure that the wind does not blow doors suddenly shut. Be especially cautious with swinging doors; a puppy may try to push one open, become caught, try to back out, and strangle. Clear glass doors may not be seen, and the puppy could be injured running into them. Never close a garage door

with your dog running about. Finally, doors leading to unfenced outdoor areas should be kept securely shut.

Peke Protection Outdoors

Your fence must not only be strong enough to keep your dog in, but to keep stray dogs out. This is why the "invisible fences" (which work by shocking a dog wearing a special receiver collar when it crosses a buried boundary wire) are not recommended for Pekingese—they don't keep other animals out. If you live in a rural area, some wild animals may look upon a Peke puppy as a snack. Still, the number one predator of any dog is the automobile. Good fences don't only make good neighbors—they make live dogs!

There can still be dangers within the yard. Bushes with sharp, broken branches at Pekingese eye level should be removed. Watch for trees with dead branches in danger of falling, or even heavy falling fruits or pine cones. If you have a pool, be aware that although dogs are natural swimmers, a Pekingese is too small to pull itself up a swimming pool wall, and can easily drown.

A Pack of Pekes?

There are certain advantages to having more than one Pekingese. Two dogs are twice the fun of one, without actually being twice the work. Consider adding another pet if you are gone for most of the day. Pekingese generally get along well with each other, although intact (unneutered) dogs of the same sex and age are apt to engage in dominance disputes. On the other hand, intact males and females together will provide you with the bi-yearly problem of keeping Romeo and Juliet separated. In many ways, three dogs can be better than two, because with two dogs a problem can arise when one is left alone while you train or give personal attention to the other. With three, there is always a pair left.

When introducing new dogs, it is best if both are taken to a neutral site so that territoriality does not provoke aggression. Two people walking the dogs beside each other as they would on a regular walk is an ideal way for dogs to accept each other.

Pekingese are more likely to be hurt by a cat than the other way around. When introducing a dog and cat, the cat should be prevented from running away, which would elicit a chase response in the dog. If the dog is fed every time the cat appears, it will associate feeding time with the cat and will come to like it. Many Pekes have become fast friends with "their" pet cats.

Packing Your Peke

The small size, calm demeanor, and desire to be by their owner's side make Pekingese natural traveling companions. You may find that sharing a trip with your Pekingese, especially if you would otherwise be traveling

A safe haven for puppy and home: the X-pen.

alone, can be a rewarding experience. But without planning, it could also be the worst trip you've ever taken, because many motels, attractions, beaches, and parks do not allow

Some Common Poisonous Ornamental or Weedy Plants
- Yew
- Mistletoe
- English holly berries
- Philodendron
- Jerusalem cherry
- Azalea
- Rhododendron
- Foxglove
- Water hemlock
- Milkweed
- Rattlebox
- Corn cockle
- Jimson weed
- Jessamine
- Oleander
- Castor bean

It's hard to have just one!

many cases they are the only self-defense establishments have against irresponsible dog owners. Even a little Pekingese can do its share of damage. Barking in motel rooms, urinating on motel rugs, defecating in walking areas, snapping at friendly passersby—the next time you are turned away from a motel with your dog, you can thank those owners who think their adorable dogs are immune from the rules. Please do not be one of them.

Riding in the Cage

Ideally your Pekingese should always ride with the equivalent of a doggy seat belt: the cage. Many dogs have emerged from their cages shaken but safe, from accidents that would have otherwise proved fatal. The least safe place for your Peke to ride is in the driver's lap or hanging its head out of the window. And always be careful that your Peke doesn't jump out of the car the minute you stop.

Carsickness

Nothing can spoil a roadtrip like a carsick dog. Carsickness is a common ailment of puppies; most outgrow it, but some need car training in order to overcome it. Initial car rides should be made extremely short, with the objective being to complete the ride before the dog gets sick. Driving to a place where the dog can get out and enjoy itself before returning home also seems to help the dog look forward to car rides and overcome carsickness. Obviously your dog shouldn't have a full stomach, but sometimes just a little food in its stomach may help. Motion sickness medication may help in stubborn cases. Consult your veterinarian.

even small pets. There are several publications listing motels that do accept dogs, and many major attractions have dog boarding facilities on their grounds, but some are not adequate for a Pekingese.

Sometimes the rules against dogs seem very unfair. Unfortunately, in

Temperature

Traveling in summer can be extremely difficult with a Pekingese. Even on relatively cool days, the

When going for a drive, allowing your dog some time to get out and play may help it to overcome carsickness.

temperature in a closed car can rise rapidly to fatally high levels. But a Pekingese can slip out of an opened window unless it is barely left open at all. Never tie a dog inside a car because it can hang itself. The best solution if you must travel in summer with your dog is to use a cage with a padlocked door (and padlocked to your car) so that you can leave the windows down. Still, if it is warm you may have to leave the car running with the air-conditioning on, which may not be the safest alternative either.

Air Travel

If your Peke is more of the jet-setter type, you may be able to carry your friend with you in the passenger compartment. Check with the airline way ahead of time to find out what size cage can fit beneath the seat, which is where your Peke would ride. Make reservations because usually there is a limit on the number of dogs allowed to ride with the passengers. If your dog cannot ride in the passenger compartment, do not allow it to fly at any time of year except winter. Although the baggage compartment where dogs ride is pressurized and heated, it is not air-conditioned and can reach high temperatures during the time the plane sits on the runway.

The Pekingese in Public

Whether you will be spending your nights at a motel, campground, or even a friend's home, always have your dog on its very best behavior. Ask beforehand if it will be OK for you to bring your Pekingese. Have your dog clean and parasite free. Do not allow your Peke pal to run loose at motels or campgrounds, and do not allow it to run helter-skelter through the homes of friends. Bring your dog's own clean blanket or bed, or better yet, its cage. Your dog will appreciate the familiar place to sleep, and it will

The cage is your Peke's best friend on the road; it provides a safe place to travel, and a secure place to rest.

keep your Pekingese out of danger. After all, you can't expect your hosts to have Peke-proofed their home like you have. Even though your dog may be used to sleeping on furniture at home, a proper dog guest stays on the floor or on its own bedding when visiting. Walk and walk your dog (and clean up after it) to make sure no accidents occur inside. Never leave your dog unattended in a strange place. The dog's perception is that you have left and forgotten it; it either barks or tries to dig its way out through the doors in an effort to find you, or becomes upset and relieves itself on the carpet. Make sure your Pekingese is so well behaved your host invites both of you back.

The Pekingese Travel Kit

The suitcase for a well-prepared Peke traveler should include:

- First aid kit
- Heartworm preventative
- Any other medications
- Food
- Food and water bowls

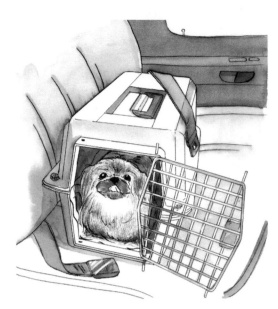

The Pekingese seatbelt is its cage, preferably itself belted into place.

- Dog biscuits and chewies
- Flea spray
- Grooming supplies
- Change of bedding
- Short and long leashes
- Flashlight
- Plastic baggies or other "poop" disposal items
- Moist towelettes
- Paper towels
- Health and rabies certificate

Beside the regular tags, your dog should wear identification indicating where you could be reached while on your trip, or including the address of someone you know will be at home. Bring a recent color photo in case your Peke somehow gets lost. If you are traveling by car, a jug of water from home can be a big help, as many dogs are very sensitive to changes in water and can develop diarrhea—the last thing you need on a trip.

Traveling with your Pekingese will take some planning, but you may find that the trip is much more enjoyable because of the presence of your most loyal travel companion.

Boarding Your Peke

Sometimes you must leave your dog behind when you travel. Ask friends or your veterinarian for boarding kennel recommendations. The ideal kennel will be approved by the American Boarding Kennel Association, have climate-controlled accommodations, and keep your Peke either indoors or in a combination indoor/outdoor run. The kennel must be air-conditioned in warm weather. Make an unannounced visit to the kennel and ask to see the facilities. While you can't expect spotlessness and a perfume atmosphere, runs should be clean and the odor should not be overpowering. Good kennels will require proof of immunizations, and an incoming check for fleas. They will allow you to bring toys and bedding, and will administer medication. Strange dogs should not be allowed to mingle, and the entire kennel area should be fenced.

Your dog may be more comfortable if an experienced pet sitter or responsible friend comes to your home and feeds and exercises your dog regularly. Whatever means you choose, always leave emergency numbers and your veterinarian's name.

Little Dog Lost

If your Pekingese escapes or gets lost, you must act quickly in order to ensure its safe return. If your dog has recently escaped, don't wait for it to show up. Immediately go to the very worst place you could imagine it going. If you live near a roadway, go there, and search backward toward your home. If you still can't find your pet, get clear pictures of your dog and go door to door. Ask any workers or delivery persons in the area if they have seen it. Call the local animal control, police department, and veterinarians. If your dog is tattooed or has been implanted with a microchip identifier (see following), contact the registry (see page 94 for telephone number). Make up large posters with a picture of a Pekingese. Take out an ad in the local paper. Mention a reward, but do not specify an amount.

A word of caution: Never give anyone reward money before seeing your dog. There are a number of scams involving answering lost dog ads, many asking for money for shipping the dog back to you from a distance or for paying veterinary bills, when very often these people have not really found your dog. If your dog is tattooed, you can have the person read the tattoo to you in order to positively identify it.

Tattoos and Microchips

Even license tags cannot always ensure your dog's return, because they must be on the dog to be effective. Tattooing your Social Security number or your dog's registration number on the inside of its ear or thigh provides a permanent means of identification. You can also have a microchip implanted with a simple injection. Microchips and tattoos are registered with pet agencies that will put you in touch with anyone who reports finding your pet. You may wish to discuss these options with your veterinarian or local breeders.

Royal Dog Food

Choosing a meal fit for a king (or queen) will be your responsibility for the life of your Peke, and your Peke's life will depend in part upon the choices you make. Dog food claims can be very confusing, but as long as you understand some essentials, you can have confidence in your decisions.

Although dogs are members of the order Carnivora ("meat-eaters"), they are actually omnivorous, meaning their nutritional needs can be met by a diet derived from both animals and plants. Most dogs do have decided preferences for meat over non-meat foods, but a balanced meal will combine both meat and plant-based nutrients.

The Porky Peke

The dog's wild ancestor, the wolf, evolved to survive feast and famine, eating huge amounts following a kill, but then perhaps waiting several days

Proper nutrition is the foundation for good health and a long life.

before another feast. In today's world, dogs can feast daily, and without the period of famine, they can easily become obese.

Pekingese are relatively little dogs. And little dogs fall victim to poor feeding practices far too often, because little dogs don't need much food. If a little dog gets a lot of food it will no longer be a little dog. If you sneak your Peke a few potato chips and the remains of your ice cream—a mere morsel for most dogs—your Peke will have very little room left for its properly balanced dog food. Add to this the Peke's demanding nature and soulful eyes, and a decided tendency for Pekingese owners to dote on their dears, and you have a recipe for obesity.

Proper Pekingese weight will depend upon the bone structure of the dog, with the sleeve Pekes weighing only a few pounds. The AKC standard dictates that no proper-sized Peke should weigh over 14 pounds (6.4 kg). It's difficult to gauge Peke weight visually, but you should be able to just feel the ribs slightly when you run your hands along the rib cage, and there should be an indication of a waistline when viewed from above, with no fat deposits around the tail base, neck, or shoulders.

If your Pekingese is overweight, try a less fattening food or feed less of your current food. Make sure also that family members aren't sneaking it tidbits. If your Peke remains overweight, seek your veterinarian's opinion. Some endocrine disorders, such as hypothyroidism or Cushing's disease (see pages 72 and 73) can cause the appearance of obesity and should be ruled out or treated, but most cases of obesity are simply from eating more calories than are expended. The Pekingese body structure should not be asked to support excessive weight; too much weight could actually prove crippling to these dogs, as well as predisposing them to joint injuries and herniated discs.

Several commercial high-fiber, low-fat, and medium-protein diet dog foods are available, which supply about 15 percent fewer calories per pound. It is preferable to feed one of these foods rather than simply feeding less of a high-calorie food.

Many people find that one of the many pleasures of dog ownership is sharing a special treat with their pet. Rather than giving up this bonding activity, substitute a low-calorie alternative such as rice cakes or carrots. Keep the dog out of the kitchen or dining area at food preparation or meal times. Schedule a walk immediately following your dinner to get your dog's mind off your leftovers—it will be good for both of you.

The Picky Peke

The Peke that turns its nose up at its dinner is another special challenge. First make sure your Peke is not snubbing its food with good reason. Many poor-quality dog foods are not particularly tasty. Pekes don't eat so much that you can't afford to buy your dog a high-quality food. If you do have an underweight dog, try feeding puppy food; add water, milk, or canned food, and heat slightly to increase aroma and palatability. Try a couple of dog food brands, but if your Peke still won't eat, you may have to employ some tough love. Many picky eaters are created when their owners begin to spice up their food with especially tasty treats. The dog then refuses to eat unless the treat is offered, and finally

The best foods will have your Pekingese dancing for its dinner because they provide good nutrition and taste.

Feeding Time

Very young puppies should be fed three or four times a day, on a regular schedule. Feed them as much as they care to eat in about 15 minutes. From the age of three to six months, pups should be fed three times daily, and after that, twice daily. Adult dogs can be fed once a day, but it is actually preferable to feed smaller meals twice a day.

Some people let the dog decide when to eat by leaving food available at all times. If you choose to let the dog "self-feed," monitor its weight to be sure it is not overindulging. Leave only dry food in the bowl as canned food spoils rapidly and becomes both unsavory and unhealthy.

Never Feed

• Chicken, pork, lamb, or fish bones. These can be swallowed and their sharp ends can pierce the esophagus, stomach, or intestinal walls.

• Any bone that could be swallowed whole. This could cause choking or intestinal blockage.

• Raw meat, which could contain *Salmonella* or other pathogens.

• Mineral supplements, unless advised to do so by your veterinarian.

• Chocolate. It contains theobromine, which is poisonous to dogs.

• Alcohol. Small dogs can drink fatal amounts quickly.

learns that if it refuses even that proffered treat, another even tastier enticement will be forthcoming. Give your Peke a good, tasty meal, but don't succumb to Pekingese blackmail or you may be a slave to your dog's gastronomical whims for years to come.

An exception, of course, is a sick dog, in which case feeding by hand is warranted. Cat food or meat baby food are both relished by dogs and may entice a dog without an appetite to eat.

The finicky Peke confronts its owner with a battle of the wills—and too often wins!

The Fine Print

The food you choose should contain a label stating that it is complete and balanced for your dog's life stage, and that it meets the standards of the American Association of Feed Control Officers (AAFCO) in *feeding trials*. The components that vary most from one brand of food to another are protein and fat percentages.

Protein: Many high-quality foods boast of being high in protein, and with good reason. Protein provides the necessary building blocks for growth and maintenance of bones and muscle, and in the production of infection-fighting antibodies. The best sources of protein are meat-based, but soybeans are also a popular source. Puppies and adolescents need particularly high protein levels in their diets, which is one reason they are best fed a food formulated for their life stage. Older dogs may need to be fed much lower levels of very high-quality protein if they are developing kidney problems, but otherwise don't usually need lowered protein. Contrary to popular belief, feeding high protein amounts doesn't cause kidney problems, but it worsens such problems if they are present.

Fat: Fat is the calorie-rich component of foods, and most dogs prefer the taste of foods with higher fat content. Fat is necessary to good health, aiding in the transport of important vitamins and providing energy. Dogs deficient in fat often have sparse, dry coats. A higher fat content is usually found in puppy foods, while obese dogs or dogs with heart problems would do well to be fed a lower fat food.

Choose a food that has a protein and fat content best suited for your dog's life stage, adjusting for any weight or health problems (prescription diets formulated for specific health problems are available). Also examine the list of ingredients: A good rule of thumb is that three or four of the first six ingredients should be animal-derived. These tend to be more palatable and more highly digestible than plant-based ingredients; more highly digestible foods mean less stool volume and fewer gas problems.

Food Types

Dry food (containing about 10 percent moisture) is the most popular, economical, and healthiest, but least palatable form of dog food. Semimoist foods (with about 30 percent moisture) contain high levels of sugar used as preservatives, which may not be good for dental health; however, they are palatable and convenient, and very handy for traveling. Pay no attention to their meatlike shapes, though; they all start out as a powder and are formed to look like meat chunks or ground beef. The high moisture content (about 75 percent) of canned foods helps to make them tasty, but it also makes them comparatively expensive, since you are in essence buying water. A steady diet of canned food would not provide the chewing necessary to maintain dental health. In addition, a high meat content tends to increase levels of dental plaque. Dog biscuits provide excellent chewing action, and some of the better varieties provide complete nutrition.

Your Pekingese will make the final decision about what food is accept-

Dog food now comes in a dizzying array of types, flavors, and specialties.

No chocolate! This is one treat that could prove fatal.

able, but some compromising may be in order. Find a food that your dog likes, one that creates a small volume of firm stools and results in good weight with a nice coat.

You may have to do a little experimenting to find just the right food, but a word of warning: One of the great mysteries of life is why a species, such as the dog, that is renowned for its lead stomach and preference to eat out of garbage cans, can at the same time develop violently upset stomachs simply from changing from one high-quality dog food to another. But it happens. So when changing foods, you should do so gradually, mixing in progressively more and more of the new food each day for several days.

The Mannered Pekingese at Home

Like any family member, your Peke needs a set of ground rules concerning what is acceptable household behavior.

Housebreaking

To avoid accidents, learn to predict when your puppy will have to relieve itself. Immediately after awakening, and soon after drinking a lot or playing, your puppy will urinate. You will probably have to carry a younger pup outside to get it to the "toilet" on time. Right after eating, or if nervous, your puppy will have to defecate. Circling, whining, sniffing, and generally acting worried usually signals that defecation is imminent. Even if the puppy starts to relieve itself, quickly but calmly scoop the pup up and carry it outside (the surprise of being picked up will usually cause the puppy to stop in midstream, so to speak). You can add a firm "No," but yelling and swatting are neither necessary nor effective. When the puppy does relieve itself at its outside toilet, remember to heap on the praise and let your Peke pup know how pleased you are.

If you are using a cage for your puppy's den, your Peke will naturally try to avoid soiling it. But puppies have very weak control over their bowels, so that if you don't take them to their elimination area often, they may not be able to avoid soiling. Further, if the cage is too large for the puppy, it may simply step away from the area in which it sleeps and relieve itself at the other end of the cage. An overly large cage can be divided with a secure barrier until the puppy is larger or housebroken.

Paper and Litter Box Training

If you cannot be with your puppy for an extended period, you may wish to leave it outside (weather permitting) so that it will not be forced to have an indoor accident. If this is not possible, you may have to paper train your puppy. Place newspapers on the far side of the room (or X-pen), away from the puppy's bed or water bowl; near a door to the outside is best. Place the puppy on the papers as soon as it starts to relieve itself. A convenient aspect of paper training is that the concept of using the paper will transfer to wherever you put the paper, so if you later take the paper outside, it can act as a training tool there. You can also litter box train your puppy. Place newspaper or even cat litter in a cat box, add some soiled newspaper or something with the scent of urine, and place the pup in the box when it begins to urinate. Apartment dwellers may find that a box-trained Pekingese is very convenient on rainy days.

Why "Accidents" Happen

No matter how wonderful and smart your Pekingese is, it probably will not have full control over its bowels until it is around six months of age. When a Peke soils the house several questions must be asked, such as, Was the dog ever really completely housebroken? If the answer is No, you must begin housebreaking anew. Sometimes a housebroken dog will be forced to soil the house because of a bout of diarrhea, and afterwards will continue to soil in the same area. If this happens, restrict that area from the dog, and revert to basic housebreaking lessons once again.

Submissive dogs may urinate upon greeting you; punishment only makes this "submissive urination" worse. Keep greetings calm, don't bend over or otherwise dominate the dog, and usually this can be outgrown.

Some dogs defecate or urinate due to the stress of separation anxiety; you must treat the anxiety to cure the symptom. Older dogs may simply not have the bladder control that they had as youngsters; paper training or a doggy door is the best solution for them. Older spayed females may "dribble." Ask your veterinarian about estrogen supplementation therapy. Younger dogs may lose bladder control due to an infection. Several small urine spots are a sign that a trip to the veterinarian is needed.

Male dogs may "lift their leg" inside the house as a means of marking it as theirs. Castration may solve this problem if done before the habit develops; otherwise, diligent disinfecting and the use of some dog-deterring deodorants may help. You can also fashion a diaper out of an old sweater sleeve for incorrigible leg lifters.

Even Pekingese Misbehave

In many breeds there are consistent complaints about particular behavioral problems. Pekingese owners seldom admit to any problems, and certainly none that is widespread in the breed. True, many are stubborn, but that seems to be one of the Peke's most endearing traits. However, despite their regal demeanor, Pekingese are still dogs, and at least occasionally share the behavioral problems to which all dogs are prone.

Even the best behaved Pekingese can succumb to temptation. Help your Peke behave by Peke-proofing your home.

Barking: Pekingese are typically very quiet dogs, but an occasional dog will decide that barking is a wonderful pastime. Isolated dogs will often bark as a means of getting attention and alleviating loneliness. Even if the attention gained includes punishment, the dog will continue to bark in order to obtain the temporary presence of the owner. The simplest solution is to move the dog's domain to a less isolated location. For example, if barking occurs when your pup is put to bed, move its bed into your bedroom. If this is not possible, the pup's quiet behavior must be rewarded by the owner's presence, working up to gradually longer and longer periods. The distraction of a special chew toy, given only at bedtime, may help alleviate barking.

The pup who must spend the day home alone is a greater challenge. Again, the simplest solution is to change the situation, perhaps by adding another animal—a good excuse to get two Pekes!

HOW-TO:
Speaking Pekingese

Extreme submissive pose.

How do you see eye to eye with a member of another species when you live in two very different worlds? You will be teaching your dog your human language; take the time to learn to speak Peke.

Translating "Peke Speak"

Like their wolf ancestors, Pekes depend upon facial expressions and body language in social interactions:

• A yawn is often a sign of nervousness. Drooling and panting can indicate extreme nervousness or motion sickness.

• A wagging tail, lowered head, and exposed teeth upon greeting is a sign of submission.

• The combination of a lowered body, wagging tucked tail, urination, and perhaps even rolling over is a sign of extreme submission.

• The combination of exposed teeth, a high, rigidly held tail, raised hackles, very upright posture, stiff-legged gait, direct stare, forward raised ears, and perhaps lifting its leg to urinate indicates very dominant, threatening behavior.

• The combination of a wagging tail, front legs and elbows on the ground and rear in the air, with or without vocalizations is the classic "play-bow" position, and is an invitation for a game.

The Pekingese conformation makes some of its body language a little more subtle than that of most other breeds. But Peke owners soon become adept at reading their friends.

A Peke's Eye View

Your Pekingese not only speaks a different language

The classic "play-bow" position.

than you do, but it lives in a different sensory world.

Olfaction: Short-nosed breeds, such as the Pekingese, have less olfactory area and fewer olfactory receptors than do longer-nosed breeds, and some researchers have proposed that they may not have quite as acute a sense of smell as longer-nosed breeds. This has not been proven, however, and, regardless, the Pekingese scenting ability is so vastly superior to ours that any small differences between breeds is hardly worth pointing out. After all, most people don't get a Pekingese with the idea of using it as a hunting dog.

Taste: Dogs also have a well developed sense of taste, and have most of the same taste receptors that we do. Research has shown that they prefer meat (not exactly earth-shaking news), and while there are many individual differences, the average dog prefers beef, pork, lamb, chicken, and horsemeat, in that order.

Dogs have sugar receptors similar to ours, which explains why many have a sweet tooth. But their perception of artificial sweeteners is not like ours, and seem to taste bitter to them.

Vision: Dogs do not see the world with as much detail or color as do humans. The dog's sense of color is like that of a "color-blind" person. That is, they confuse similar shades of yellow-green, yellow, orange, and red, but can readily see and discriminate blue, indigo, and violet from all other colors and each other.

The dog's vision is superior when it comes to seeing in very dim light. The eyeshine you may see from your dog's eyes at night is from a structure that serves to increase its ability to see in the dark.

Hearing: Dogs can hear much higher tones than humans can, and so can be irritated by high hums from your TV or from those ultrasonic flea collars. The Peke's drop ears may somewhat encumber its sense of hearing, but the effect is very small.

Pain: Many people erroneously believe that animals cannot feel pain, but common sense and scientific research indicate that dogs and other animals have a well-developed sense of pain. Many dogs are amazingly stoic, however, and their ability to deal with pain is not totally understood at present. Because a dog may not be able to express that it is in pain, you must be alert to

The nervous dog will pant, drool, and shake, as well as hold its ears back and down.

changes in your dog's demeanor. A stiff gait, low head carriage, reluctance to get up, irritability, dilated pupils, whining, or limping are all indications that your dog is in pain.

Separation anxiety is characterized by lapses in housebreaking, nervous behavior, and destruction around doors and windows, i.e., chewed and scratched walls, door jams, and rugs.

Digging and chewing: Many a Pekingese owner has returned home to a scene of carnage and suspected that some mad dog must have broken into the house and gone berserk; after all, that quiet little Pekingese could never wreak such havoc. Never underestimate a determined Pekingese!

Adult dogs may dig or destroy items through frustration or boredom. The best way to deal with these dogs is to provide both physical interaction (such as chasing a ball) and mental interaction (such as practicing a few simple obedience commands) on a daily basis.

One of the most common causes of destructive behavior is also one of the most misunderstood: separation anxiety. Some normally sedate Pekingese turn into demolition dogs when left alone. The owners attribute this Jekyll and Hyde behavior to the dog "spiting" them for leaving, or think that their dog only misbehaves then because it knows it would be caught otherwise.

But an observant owner will notice some things that are different about the dog that destroys only when left alone. For one, the dog often appears to be in a highly agitated state when the owner returns. For another, the sites of destruction are often around doors, windows, or fences, suggestive of an attempt to escape. Such dogs are reacting to the anxiety of being left alone—remember that for a social animal this is a highly stressful situation, but the average owner, upon returning home to such ruin, punishes the dog. This in no way alleviates the anxiety of being left alone; it does, however, eventually create anxiety associated with the owner's return home, and this tends to escalate the destructive behavior. Dogs seem to understand "when the house is in shreds and my owner appears, I get punished," but not to understand "when I chew the house it gets messed up and I will be punished when my owner appears." If they did, punishment would remedy the problem. It does not. Instead, owners must realize that they are dealing with a fear response—the fear of being alone.

The foolhardiness of punishing a dog for being afraid should be obvious. Instead of punishing the dog, it must be conditioned to overcome its fear of separation. This is done by separating the dog for very short periods of time and gradually working up to longer periods, taking care to never allow the dog to become anxious during any session. This is complicated when the owner *must* leave the dog for long periods during the conditioning program. In these cases, the part of the house or yard in which the dog is left for long periods should be different from the part in which the conditioning sessions take place; the latter location should be the location in which the owner wishes to leave the dog after conditioning is completed. In either case, when the owner returns home, no matter what the condition of the home, greet the dog calmly or even ignore it for a few minutes, to emphasize the point that being left was really no big deal. Then have the dog perform a simple trick or obedience exercise so that you have an excuse to praise it. It takes a lot of patience, and often a whole lot of self-control, but it's not fair to you or your dog to let this situation continue.

Fearfulness: A bold breed by nature, nonetheless an occasional Peke can be wary of strangers, other dogs, or loud noises. Never push your dog into situations that might overwhelm it. A program of gradual desensitization, with the dog exposed to the frightening person or thing and then rewarded for calm behavior, is time-consuming but the best way to alleviate the fear. Never force a dog who is afraid of strangers to be petted by somebody it doesn't know; it in no way helps the dog overcome its fear and is a good way for the stranger to get bitten. Strangers should be asked to ignore shy dogs, even when approached by the dog. Dogs seem to fear the attention of a stranger more than they fear the strangers themselves.

Never coddle your dog when it acts afraid, because it reinforces the behavior. It is always useful if your Pekingese knows a few simple commands; performing these exercises correctly gives you a reason to praise the dog and also increases the dog's sense of security because it knows what is expected of it (see the commands beginning on page 50). Whether it is a fear of strangers, other dogs, car rides, thunder, or being left alone, the concept is the same—never hurry, and never push the dog to the point that it is afraid.

Aggression: Pekingese are not typically aggressive dogs, but an occasional Peke will behave more aggressively than is socially acceptable.

Humans and dogs have formed the most intriguing partnership; living in two different worlds, but sharing each other's lives.

The best cure for aggression is prevention, and the best prevention is to carefully select your Pekingese from a responsible breeder. Then teach your Peke to look forward to guests by rewarding proper behavior, such as sitting and staying, in the guests' presence. Have the guest offer the dog a tidbit when it acts in a civil fashion. Some Pekes will bite out of resentment, perhaps because they are always hustled out of the house when company arrives, or in the presence of a new baby. Again, the solution is to teach your dog to respond to simple commands such as sit and stay, and use them to help the dog be well mannered in the presence of guests or babies. In drastic cases, attention can be withheld from the dog except in the presence of guests or babies, so that the dog associates being with them as something that brings itself attention and rewards. Of course, it should hardly be mentioned that no baby or child should be allowed to play roughly with or tease your Peke; one could hardly blame a Pekingese that growls or bites out of

Welcome home! No matter how upset you may feel, ignore the dog when you come home. Punishment won't help separation anxiety.

self-defense, but one could blame its owner for letting the situation develop.

Unlike in humans, where direct eye contact is seen as a sign of sincerity, staring a dog directly in the eye is interpreted by the dog as a threat. It can cause a fearful dog to bite out of what it perceives as self-defense.

Aggression between dogs within a household is seldom a problem with Pekes, but it can be serious when it does occur. Dogs may be vying for dominance, and fights will occur until one dog emerges as the clear victor. Even in cases where one dog is dominant, fights may erupt when both are competing for the owner's attention. The dominant dog expects to get that attention before the subordinate, but being fair-minded owners, we tend to give attention equally, or to even favor the "under-dog." This can be interpreted by the dominant dog as an uprising by the subordinate dog, who is then attacked. This is one case where playing favorites (to the dominant dog) will actually be a favor to the subordinate dog in the long run!

Coprophagia: Few dogs are more difficult to comprehend than those that stick their noses up at gourmet dog food and then sneak a feast from the cat's litter box at the first opportunity. But the sad (and unappetizing) truth is that all dogs, Pekes included, consider cat, rabbit, and various livestock feces a special delicacy. Just do your best to keep the litter box out of reach and realize that dogs aren't quite so human as we would like to believe!

Less tolerable is the dog that eats its own feces. A number of theories have been advanced to explain this most repulsive of eating habits—boredom, nutritional deficiency, filth—but none is adequate to explain all instances. Food additives are available to make the stool less savory, but the best cure is prevention by fastidious poop-scooping. Many dogs experiment with feces-eating as pups, but most will outgrow it.

At Wit's End

Chances are you and your Pekingese will live together blissfully with never a major behavioral problem. But if a problem does arise that you are unable to solve, consult your veterinarian. Some problems have physiological bases that can be treated. Also, your veterinarian may refer you to a specialist in canine behavior problems.

To Train a Lion Dog

Independent and stubborn, the typical Pekingese is not the ideal candidate for Lassie's next understudy. Training with the same techniques as those used for the typical waggy-tailed, boisterous, lick-your-boots breed is a recipe for failure. In fact, training a Peke means walking a fine line between keeping the upper hand but sometimes letting the dog think it is training you!

Most breeds have difficulty mastering their impulses for perpetual motion, but not so the Peke. It is already calm, and will learn the down/stay before any other dog in its obedience class. But it will also learn to be bored and to lag behind while heeling before any other dog in the class. And when it plants its feet and refuses to move, you can appreciate the description of the Peke as weighing far more than it would appear. Whether you want an obedience star or a well-mannered pet, there are certain concepts that every good trainer should know, and certain commands that every good Pekingese should know.

What Every Good Pekingese Trainer Should Know

Successful Pekingese trainers all emphasize that Pekes must be trained with a firm but gentle touch. Remember the following rules of Pekingese training:

Gently guide: Pekes want to please but they don't want to be ordered. Tough, domineering training techniques are more likely to bring out the stubborn streak in a Peke as it plants all fours and just quits playing this game of yours until you decide to shape up.

Never rough: Such methods as striking, shaking, choking, and even hanging have been touted by some (stupid) trainers. Do not try them! They are extremely dangerous, counterproductive, and cruel. They have no place in the training of a beloved family member. Pekingese are a sensitive breed both mentally and physically, and seldom require anything but the mildest of corrections. A direct stare with a harsh "NO!" should be all that is required in almost any instance.

The correct placement of the choke collar is with the long end (to which the lead is attached) coming over the top of the dog's head from the dog's left to right side. Note: For illustrative purposes, the collar is shown here larger than would be desirable for a Pekingese.

The well-trained dog gains confidence and enjoys life more because it is trusted to behave in all situations. Training your Peke is the best gift you can give it.

Correct and be done with it: Owners sometimes try to make this "a correction the dog will remember" by ignoring the dog for the rest of the day. The dog may indeed remember that its owner ignored it, but it will not remember why. Again, the dog can only relate its present behavior to your actions.

Food is forever: There is nothing wrong with using food as a reward *as long as you intend to continue using it.* If you train a dog using food to tell it that it has done well, and then stop rewarding it with food, the impression to the dog is that it has no longer done well. It may eventually quit performing altogether under these circumstances. If you do use food, precede it with praise; that is, praise, then give the dog a tidbit. Also, don't reward with food every time; keep the dog wondering if this will be the time with the tidbit payoff (the slot machine philosophy of dog training). That way, when you can't reward with a treat, your Peke will not be surprised and will continue to per-

form in the absence of food for comparatively long periods. Of course, the advantage of using praise rather than food is that you never can be caught without praise available.

Be consistent: Sometimes a Pekingese can be awfully cute when it misbehaves, or sometimes your hands are full, and sometimes you just aren't sure what you want from your dog. But lapses in consistency are ultimately unfair to the dog. If you feed your Peke from the table because it begs "just this one time," you have taught it that while begging may not always result in a handout, you never know—it just might pay off tonight. In other words, *you* have taught your dog to beg.

Train before meals: Your dog will work better if its stomach is not full, and will be more responsive to treats if you use them as rewards. Never try to train a sleepy, tired, or hot Pekingese.

Happy endings: Begin and end each training session with something the dog can do well. And keep sessions short and fun—no longer than 10 to 15 minutes. Dogs have short attention spans and you will notice that after about 15 minutes their performance will begin to suffer unless a lot of play is involved. To continue to train a tired or bored dog will result in the training of bad habits, resentment in the dog, and frustration for the trainer. Especially when training a young puppy, or when you only have one or two different exercises to practice, quit while you are ahead! Keep your Pekingese wanting more, and you will have a happy, willing, obedience partner.

Name first: The first ingredient in any command is your dog's name. You probably spend a good deal of your day talking, with very few words intended as commands for your dog. So warn your Pekingese that this talk is directed toward it.

Then command: Many trainers make the mistake of simultaneously saying the command word *at the same time* that they are placing the dog into position. *This is incorrect.* The command comes immediately *before* the desired action or position. The crux of training is anticipation: the dog comes to anticipate that after hearing a command, it will be induced to perform some action, and it will eventually perform this action without further assistance from you. On the other hand, when the command and action come at the same time, not only does the dog tend to pay more attention to your action of placing it in position, and less attention to the command word, but the command word loses its predictive value for the dog. Remember: Name, command, action, reward!

Once is enough: Repeating a word over and over, or shouting it louder and louder, never helped anyone, dog or human, understand what is expected of them. Your Peke is not hard of hearing.

Say what you mean and mean what you say: Your Pekingese takes its commands literally. If you have taught that "Down" means to lie down, then what must the dog think when you yell "Down" to tell it to get off the sofa where it was already lying down? If "Stay" means not to move until given a release word, and you say "Stay here" as you leave the house for work, do you really want your dog to sit by the door all day until you get home?

Think like a dog: In many ways dogs are like young children; they act to gratify themselves, and they often do so without thinking ahead to consequences. But unlike young children, dogs cannot understand human language (except for those words you teach them), so you cannot explain to them that their actions of five minutes earlier were bad. Dogs live in the present; if you punish them, they can only assume it is for their behavior at the time of punishment. So if you discover

a mess, drag your dog to it from its nap in the other room, and scold, the impression to the dog will be that either it is being scolded for napping, or that its owner is mentally unstable. Remember, timing is everything in a correction. If you discover your dog in the process of having an "accident," and snatch the dog up and deposit it outside, and then yell "No," your dog can only conclude that you have yelled "No" to it for eliminating outside. Correct timing would be "No," quickly take the dog outside, and then praise it once it eliminates outside. In this way you have corrected the dog's undesired behavior and helped the dog understand desired behavior.

Not by the book: Finally, nothing will ever go just as perfectly as it seems to in all of the training instructions. But although there may be setbacks, you can train your dog, as long as you remember to be consistent, firm, gentle, realistic, and most of all, patient.

Pekingese Keys to Success

A big problem when training a little dog is how to guide and correct it. If you bend down to position your Pekingese every time you want it to sit, you will probably have a bad back before you have a sitting dog. Try some of these small dog solutions:
• Teach stationary exercises on a tabletop or other raised surface. This allows you to have eye contact with your dog and gives you a better vantage from which to help your dog learn.
• To train your dog at your feet, extend your arm length with a back scratcher with which to guide and even pet your dog without having to bend over.
• A leash that comes from several feet overhead has virtually no guiding ability whatsoever. You need a lower pivot point for the leash in relation to the dog, and you can achieve this by what is called a "solid leash." This is simply

Small dog training aids: a section of PVC pipe with a leash strung through it, and a light weight backscratcher or stick.

49

Use a solid lead and backscratcher to extend your reach to Pekingese level.

a hollow, light tube, such as PVC pipe, about 3 feet (0.9 m) long, through which you string your leash.
• To prevent a small dog from sitting or lying down, loop part of your regular

If your dog tends to sit when you want it to stand, try looping the lead around its belly until it gets the idea.

leash around its belly and hold onto that part, so you have a convenient "handle."

Training Equipment

The lead: Besides the backscratcher and solid leash, equipment for training should include a 6-foot (1.8 m) and a 15-foot (4.6 m) lightweight lead. For puppies (as well as shy or easily trained dogs) it is convenient to use one of the light-weight adjustable-size show leads.

The choke collar: Many Pekes can be trained with a buckle collar, but a choke collar is also an acceptable choice as long as you know how to use it correctly. *A choke collar is not for choking!* The proper way to administer a correction with a choke collar is with a gentle snap, then immediate release. If you think of the point of the correction as being to startle the dog by the sound of the chain links moving, rather than to choke or in any way hurt your dog, you will be correcting with the right level of force, and won't risk hurting your Peke's neck. The choke collar is placed on the dog so that the ring with the lead attached comes up around the left side of the dog's neck, and through the other ring. If put on backwards, it will not release itself after being tightened (since you will be on the right side of your dog for most training). The choke collar should *never* be left on your Pekingese after a training session—there are too many tragic cases where a choke collar really did earn its name after being snagged on a fence, bush, or even a playmate's tooth.

What Every Good Pekingese Should Know

It's never too early or too late to start the education of your Pekingese. With a very young Peke, train for even shorter time periods. By the time your Peke pup (here named "Kitty") reaches six months of age, it should be familiar with the following commands:

Sit: Because Pekes are already close to the ground, many of them virtually teach themselves to sit as a means of being more comfortable while looking up at you. But you can hasten the process by holding a tidbit above your puppy's eye level, saying "Kitty, Sit," and then moving the tidbit toward your pup until it is slightly behind and above her eyes. When the puppy begins to look up and bend her hind legs, praise, then offer the tidbit. Repeat this, requiring the dog to bend her legs more and more until she must be sitting before receiving praise. This is a much more pleasant way for your puppy to learn her first lesson than the traditional push-pull method of teaching. You can help her along with a little push on her hind end, or if she hasn't gotten the hint at all, then fold her into a sit by pushing forward behind her "knees" while at the same time pushing back and up under her chin.

"Watch Me": A common problem when training any dog is that the dog's attention is elsewhere. You can teach your dog to pay attention to you by teaching it the "watch me" command. With your Pekingese sitting, say "watch me," and when it looks in your direction, give it a treat or other reward. Gradually require the dog to look at you for longer and longer periods before rewarding it. Teach "watch me" before going on to the other commands.

Stay: Next comes the "stay" command. Have your dog sit, then say "stay" in a soothing voice (you do not have to precede the "stay" command with the dog's name because you should already have your dog's attention). If your Peke attempts to get up or lie down, gently place it back into position. After only a few seconds, give a release word ("ok!"), and praise. Next, step out (starting with your right foot) and turn to stand directly in front of your dog while it stays. Work up to longer times, and then back away and

Teach tricks by guiding your Peke with a small treat. To teach "sit up," hold the treat over your Peke's head and give it to it as soon as it sits up. Then gradually require it to sit up longer before rewarding it. But don't ask it to sit up for too long; the Peke is not really built for this position.

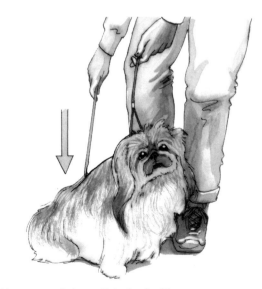

You can remind your Peke to sit with a slight tap on the rump with the backscratcher.

A hesitant youngster can be encouraged to come by dropping to its level and encouraging it to run into your waiting arms.

distances in very small increments. Don't ask a young puppy to sit for more than 30 seconds at most. When the dog does move out of position, return and calmly place it back, repeating "stay"; then return to your position, then return to the dog while it is still staying so that you can praise it. Many trainers make the mistake of staring intently at their dog during the "stay," but this is perceived by the dog as a threat and often intimidates them so that they squirm out of position.

Come: When both "sit" and "stay" are mastered, you are ready to introduce "come." Your puppy probably already knows how to come; after all, it comes when it sees you with the food bowl, or perhaps with the leash or a favorite toy. You may have even used the word "come" to get its attention then; if so, you have a head start. You want your puppy to respond to "Kitty, come" with the same enthusiasm as though you were setting down her supper; in other words, "come" should always be associated with good things.

Never have your dog come to you and then scold it for something it has done. In the dog's mind it is being scolded for coming, not for any earlier misdeed.

repeat the process. If you have been training on a table, make the transition to the floor before backing away from the dog. The object is not to push your dog to the limit, but to let it succeed. To do this, you must be very patient, and you must increase your times and

To teach the command "come," have your Peke sit, and with leash attached, command "stay" and step out to the end of the leash and face your dog. This "stay" will be a little different for your puppy, as you will drop to your knees, open your arms, and invite her with an enthusiastic "Kitty, come!" This is obviously not an exercise for tabletop training. An unsure pup can be coaxed with a tug on the lead or the sight of a tidbit. Remember to really praise; after all, you have enticed her to break the "stay" command, and she may be uneasy about that. During the training for "come," it is not unusual for there to be some regression in the performance of "stay"

Make coming fun!

due to confusion; just be gentle, patient, and consistent and this will sort itself out.

The next step is to again place the pup in the "sit/stay," walk to the end of the lead, call "Kitty, come," and quickly back away several steps, coaxing the dog to you. Eventually you can go to a longer line, and walk quickly backwards as far as your equilibrium will allow. This encourages the pup to come at a brisk pace; in fact, most dogs will regard this as an especially fun game! Of course, in real life the dog is seldom sitting when you want it to come, so once it understands what you mean by come, allow the pup to walk on lead, and at irregular intervals call "Kitty, come," run backwards, and when she reaches you, be sure to praise. Finally, attach a longer line to the pup, allow her to meander about, and in the midst of her investigations, call, walk backwards, and praise.

"Come" is the most important command your dog will ever learn. As your dog gets older you will want to practice it in the presence of distractions, such as other leashed dogs, unfamiliar people, cats, and cars. Always practice on lead. If it takes a tidbit as a reward to get your Peke motivated, then this is an instance where you should use an occasional food reward. Coming on command is more than a cute trick— it could save your dog's life.

Down: When you need your Peke to stay in one place for any long periods of time it is best for it to be left in a "down/stay." Begin teaching the "down" command with the dog in the sitting position, which, for a Peke, is only inches from the "down" position! If you are using food rewards, command "Kitty, down," then show her a tidbit and move it below her nose toward the ground. If she reaches down to get it, give it to her. Repeat, requiring her to reach farther down (without lifting her rear from the ground) until she has to

Pekes are surprisingly adept "circus-dogs."

lower her elbows to the ground. You can help her out here by easing her front legs out in front of her with your other hand.

If treats don't work, you can also gently slide your Peke's legs out in front of it in order to teach "down."

If you do not wish to use food rewards, again start with the dog sitting, command "Kitty, down," then place your left hand over her shoulders and with your right hand gently grasp both front legs and ease her to the ground. Never try to cram your dog into the down position, which could not only cause injuries, but scare a submissive dog and cause a dominant dog to resist.

Practice the "down/stay" just as you did the "sit/stay." In fact your Peke now has quite a repertoire of behaviors that you can combine in different ways to combat boredom. The only thing left for any well-behaved Pekingese is the ability to walk politely on lead.

Heel: Although in many public situations it is safer and more convenient to carry your Peke, your dog should still know how to walk nicely on a leash. Walking an untrained Pekingese can be a danger to itself and its owner as it darts underfoot and causes its owner to trip.

Your pup should already be acquainted with a lightweight leash at least by the time it has learned "come." Still, walking alongside of you on lead is a new experience for a puppy, and many will freeze in their tracks once they discover their freedom is being violated. In this case, do not simply drag the pup along, but coax it with praise—and if need be—food, until it's walking somewhere...anywhere. When the puppy follows you, praise and reward. In this way, the pup comes to realize that following you while walking on lead pays off.

Some Peke pups will bound along with delight at this new game, while others dig in their heels and appear glued to the ground. With the latter, make sure the pup is accustomed to wearing a puppy collar, and then have it wear the light leash around the house for several periods a day *while under supervision*. When it is walking and tolerating the dragging leash, pick up the leash and follow the pup around, all the while giving it an occasional tidbit. Then give a tug and a tidbit. There will be a time when you will despair of your dog ever walking on lead, but be assured that, although it may take a couple of weeks of practice everyday, your dog will eventually be strolling alongside you.

Once your Peke walks confidently on lead, it is time to ask for more. Using the solid leash, have your Peke sit in the "heel" position; that is, on your left side with its neck next to and parallel with your leg. Say "Kitty, heel" and step off with your left foot first. (Remember that you stepped off on your right foot when you left your dog on a "stay"; if you are consistent, the foot that moves first will provide an eye-level cue for your little dog.) During your first few practice sessions you will keep her on a short lead, holding her in heel position, and of course praising her. When you stop, have her sit. Although some trainers advocate letting the dog lunge to the end of the lead and then snapping it back, such an approach is unfair if you haven't shown the dog what is expected of it at first, and such methods are not appropriate for a Pekingese. Nor is the suggestion of allowing the dog to get in front of you and then stepping on it. That's not safe for either of you, nor does it foster a happy working dog. Instead, after a few sessions of showing the dog the heel position, give her a little more loose lead; if she stays in the heel position, praise; more likely she will not, in which case pull her back to position with a quick gentle tug, then release, of the lead. If, after a few days of practice, your dog still seems oblivious to your efforts, turn unexpectedly several times; teach your dog that it is its responsibility to keep an eye on you.

Keep up a pace that requires your Pekingese to walk fairly briskly; too slow a pace gives dogs time to sniff, look all around, and in general become distracted; a brisk pace will focus the dog's attention upon you and generally aid training. As you progress, you will want to add some right, left, and about-faces, and walk at all different speeds. Then practice in different areas (still always on lead) and around different distractions. Vary your routine to combat boredom, and keep training sessions short.

Mind Games

While sitting and staying and the like are necessary for good manners, they don't exactly astound your friends. For that you need something flashy, some incredible feat of intelligence and dexterity—a dog trick. Try the standards: roll over, play dead, catch, sit up, speak. All are easy to teach with the help of the same obedience concepts outlined in the training section. You will find that your particular dog is more apt to perform in ways that make some tricks easier than others to teach. Most Pekingese are easy to teach to "roll over"; give the command when the dog is already on its back, then guide the dog the rest of the way over with a treat. If your dog can physically do it, you can teach it when to do it. Some Pekes enjoy showing off, but others make it clear that such juvenile tricks are beneath their dignity.

Higher Education

Is your Pekingese "gifted?" Perhaps you would like to take it to obedience classes, where both of you can learn even more, practice around distractions, and discuss training problems with people who have similar interests. The AKC or your local Humane Society can direct you to local obedience clubs or classes. The Pekingese Club of America may also be able to direct you to Pekingese obedience enthusiasts. Attend a local obedience trial (contact the AKC for date and location) and ask local owners of happy working dogs (especially Pekes) where they train. Be forewarned that a Pekingese is not a retriever; don't expect it to wag its tail in glee for no apparent reason while it goes through its paces. This doesn't mean that the Pekingese can't enjoy obedience—it just has a more subtle way of showing it. Be aware that not all instructors may understand the Pekingese psyche, and not all classes may be right for you and your Peke.

You may wish to enter an obedience trial eventually, in which case the advice of fellow competitors will be invaluable. Obedience competitors love their sport; they love to welcome newcomers, and they love to see them succeed. Most of all, they love their dogs and understand how you love yours. Pekingese are a somewhat uncommon sight in the obedience rings, so prepare to impress a lot of onlookers who may have scoffed at the thought of a performing Peke.

In the Peak of Condition

The Lion's Mane

The Peke's crowning glory, that majestic mane and coat, needs a short grooming session about twice a week if it is to remain in all its glory. Many dogs and owners look forward to such grooming sessions as a relaxing time of bonding. The upkeep of a Pekingese requires a little grooming often, rather than a lot of grooming seldom.

Grooming even the lushest of coats requires only a wide-tooth comb, natural bristle brush, and a water spritzer bottle. You may wish to use a grooming table or other raised surface, but it is equally effective to have the dog lie on your lap while being brushed.

If you start by grooming your puppy before it's had time to develop any tangles, your pup will come to think of being brushed as something that feels

wonderful. Keep each session short, fun, and rewarding. With the young puppy, you need not follow the full grooming routine; remember, although you certainly want to prevent the formation of any tangles, your most important long-term goal now is training the pup to be cooperative. Hold the pup on your lap and accustom it to being petted or brushed, not only while it is right side up, but also while lying on its back. The fluffy puppy coat is actually more prone to matting than is the adult coat, especially at the transitional period from puppy to adult coat.

Hair and Hygiene: Peke pups sprout hair rapidly, and some of it grows in inopportune areas. The hair around the anus and the end of the sheath of the penis can accumulate waste matter. If this is a problem, you can carefully scissor the hair from these delicate regions. Even so, you will need to check these areas every time your Peke returns from relieving itself.

The feet: A typical and desirable trait of the Peke coat is the long hair of the feet. Sometimes the hair on the bottom of the feet can cause a dog to slip on a slick floor, and you may want to carefully scissor that hair so that the pads can provide traction.

The face: Your puppy must also allow you to clean its face regularly. The skin in the wrinkle over the nose should be cleaned with witch hazel and dried once or twice daily using a cotton ball. A pinch of cornstarch applied to the wrinkle can aid in keeping it dry. If left unattended, moisture will accumulate and ultimately lead to a very unpleasant odor and possibly infection. Any discharge from the eyes

Good genes and good care are the recipe for a magnificent Peke.

should be wiped away with a moist cotton ball. Cleaning your Peke's face should become a routine for the entirety of your Peke's life.

Brushing

The Pekingese is blessed with a thick double coat, consisting of a soft, fine undercoat for warmth and a longer, coarse weather-resistant overcoat. Some people make the mistake of brushing only the outer coat, inadvertently allowing the undercoat to mat. For this reason you must brush the coat in layers, taking care that the hair is brushed all the way down to the skin.

Begin brushing at the face, moving to the rear on one side of the dog, and then the other. Finally, turn the dog over and brush the underside. Before brushing, mist the coat with a light spray of water or coat conditioner. This helps prevent static electricity and lessens coat breakage. After brushing, repeat the process using the wide-tooth comb, to make sure that no tangles remain.

As your finishing touch, mist the coat again and brush the hair on the top of the body from the skull back to the end of the tail in the direction of hair growth. Brush all of the hair in the rear half of the dog (all areas behind the rib cage) in the direction of growth. The exception is the coat on the backs of the thighs, which should be brushed upward. The coat on the sides of the body over the rib cage and on the forechest should also be brushed up and forward, emphasizing the width of the chest. Finally, place the tail over the back and brush the hair in the direction of growth, which will now be toward the head.

Some cornstarch sprinkled into the coat and brushed out can help the hair to fluff, and is especially useful for the areas behind the ears, on the tail, and hind leg hair, but repeated use can dry the hair.

A grooming table is convenient but not necessary.

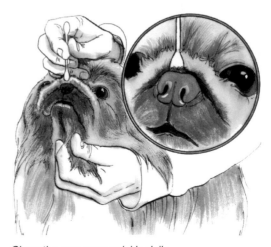

Clean the over-nose wrinkle daily.

Coat Disasters

- Wet or muddy hair can be dried and cleaned by sprinkling a liberal amount of cornstarch, rubbing it in, and brushing it out.
- Pine tar can be loosened with hair spray.
- Other tar can be worked out with vegetable oil, followed by dishwashing detergent.
- Tight mats and burrs can be helped by soaking them for an hour in tangle remover or vegetable oil.
- Chewing gum can be eased out by first applying ice.
- Skunk odor can be partially washed away with tomato juice.

Mats: You may discover some matting behind the ears or under the elbows. The coat is more prone to mat during shedding season or when it is oily or dirty. Never wash a matted coat, which only causes the mat to become more tightly bound. Try to split a mat with your fingers, starting near either end and pulling it in half longitudinally. Hold the hair between the mat and your dog's skin to avoid painful pulling. More stubborn mats may require split-

ting with a rake (a wooden brush with hard metal teeth), or, as a last resort, scissors. Even with scissors, split the mat into halves; don't just cut it out. To avoid accidentally cutting the skin, wriggle a fine comb between the mat and the skin before you start snipping.

Shedding: This is controlled not by exposure to warmer temperatures, but by exposure to longer periods of light. This is why indoor dogs, which are exposed to artificial light, tend to shed somewhat all year. Pekes have a heavier shedding session once a year, or following every estrus in females, during which time the flying hairs and matting can be overwhelming. Brush every day.

When matting is extensive or fleas are overwhelming, shaving the coat may be the only alternative. It is sometimes argued that a dog's coat acts as insulation and helps keep the dog cool in summer, but as long as the coat is not shaved to the skin, little insulation will be lost.

Bathing: The two cardinal rules of bathing are: **1.** never bathe a matted coat; and **2.** never bathe a shedding coat unless you have first brushed out every loose hair.

Dirty and oily hair has an unpleasant smell and is more likely to matt. Frequent grooming will lessen the need for frequent bathing. For the average well-kept Peke, there should be no need to bathe more than once every couple of months.

You will get better results with a shampoo made for dogs. Dog skin has a pH of 7.5, while human skin has a pH of 5.5; thus, bathing in a shampoo formulated for the pH of human skin can lead to scaling and irritation. Most shampoos will kill fleas even if not especially formulated as a flea shampoo, but none has any residual killing action on fleas. Therapeutic shampoos are available to aid skin problems. Dry, scaly skin is treated with moisturizing

The basics: comb, brush, and spritzer bottle.

shampoos, excessive scale and dandruff with antiseborrheic shampoos, damaged skin with antimicrobials, and itchy skin with oatmeal-based antipruritics. Finally, all Peke owners should have on hand one of the shampoos that requires no water or rinsing. These are wonderful for puppies, spot baths, emergencies, and bathing when time does not permit.

Even the most devoted of owners seldom look forward to bathtime. Unfortunately, most owners train their dogs to hate baths through improper early bath training. They put off giving a bath, and when they do, they figure that by making it a thorough bath, the results will somehow last longer. The secret is to give lots of tiny baths, so tiny the puppy doesn't have a chance to get scared. Rinse (don't even wash) one leg today, an ear tomorrow, and so on. Be firm, soothing, and playful. A sink with a hand-held spray is most convenient.

Once you have worked up to a full-scale bath, begin with a thorough brushing to remove tangles and distribute oils; then wet your dog down, working forward from the rear. Use water that would be comfortable for you to bathe in, and be sure to keep some running on your hand in order to monitor any temperature changes. A fractious Peke could inadvertently hit a faucet knob and cause itself to be scalded. If you keep one hand on your dog's neck or ear, it is less likely to splatter you with a wet dog shake.

Once soaked, use your hand or a soft brush to work in the shampoo (it will go a lot farther and be easier to apply if you first mix the shampoo with warm water). Pay special attention to the oily area around the ear base, but avoid getting water in the dog's ears (try plugging them with cotton). Rinse thoroughly, this time working from the head back. A cream rinse is seldom necessary, and tends to make the coat less puffy.

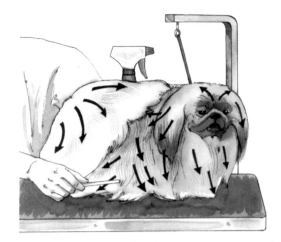

The finished coat is combed in such a way as to emphasize its fullness.

When towel drying, be sure not to rub to the point of creating tangles. The coat will look even better if you blow it dry while brushing the hair backwards. Again, you must accustom your dog to a blow dryer gradually, and always keep your hand at the place on the dog you are drying; once your hand gets uncomfortably hot, you know the dog's skin must also be uncomfortable.

Skin and Coat Problems

Skin problems in all dogs are the most common problems seen by veterinarians, and the most common of all skin problems is *flea allergy dermatitis* (FAD). Itchy, crusted bumps with hair loss in the region around the rump, especially at the base of the tail, result from a flea bite anywhere on the dog's body.

Besides FAD, dogs can have allergic reactions to pollens or other inhaled allergens. Food allergies can also occur, but are uncommon.

Pyoderma, with pus filled bumps and crusting, is another common skin disease. *Impetigo* is characterized by

By wrapping wax paper around the long ear fringes, and then folding the wrapped hair and securing it with rubber bands, the ears will not trail in food or otherwise become damaged. The long hair of the britches can also be wrapped.

such bumps and crusting most often in the groin area of puppies. Both are treated with antibiotics and antibacterial shampoos.

A reddened moist itchy spot that suddenly appears is most likely a "hot spot," which arises from an itch-scratch-chew cycle resulting most commonly from fleas or flea allergy. Clip the surrounding hair, wash the area with an oatmeal-based shampoo, and prevent the dog from further chewing. A distasteful product such as Bitter Apple may dissuade the dog from chewing, but you may have to resort to an Elizabethan collar to stop the dog from chewing itself. Your veterinarian can also prescribe antiinflammatory medication.

In *seborrhea*, there may be excessive dandruff or greasiness, often with a great deal of ear wax and a rancid odor. Treatment is with antiseborrheic shampoos.

Hair may be lost due to *hypothyroidism*, *Cushing's syndrome*, ovarian cysts, or testicular tumors. The

Pekingese is a breed predisposed to such tumors, especially in a nondescended testicle.

Pekingese Fleas

Not only are fleas terribly uncomfortable for the dog, but scratching can lead to matting, hair loss, and eye abrasions. Fleas leave behind a black pepper-like substance (actually flea feces) that turns red upon getting wet. Any flea control program must be undertaken with care, because overzealous and uninformed efforts can lead to the death of pets as well as fleas.

Insecticides are categorized as organics, natural pesticides, cholinesterase inhibitors, insect growth regulators, and systemics. Incidentally, the ultrasonic flea repelling collars have been shown to be both ineffective on fleas and irritating to dogs. Scientific studies have also shown that feeding dogs brewer's yeast or garlic, as has been advocated for years by many dog owners, is ineffective against fleas.

Organics (e.g., D-Limonene) break down the outer shell of the flea and cause death from dehydration. They are safe, but slow acting, and have no residual action. Diatomaceous earth also acts on this same principle; some researchers have expressed concern that breathing its dust can be dangerous to dogs, however, a special concern when dealing with a dog that is low to the ground. Natural grade diatomaceous earth is safer than pool grade, which is more finely ground, but neither should be used excessively.

Natural pesticides (e.g., Pyrethrin, Permethrin, Rotenone) are relatively safe and kill fleas quickly, but have a very short residual action. They do not remain in the dog's system and so can be used frequently.

Cholinesterase inhibitors (Dursban, Diazinon, malathion, Sevin, Carbaryl)

act on the nervous systems of fleas, dogs, and humans. They are used in yard sprays, dog sprays and dips, flea collars, and systemics. They kill effectively and have fairly good residual action but they can poison the dog if overused, and should never be used on puppies or sick dogs.

The systemics (Pro-Spot, Spotton) are cholinesterase inhibitors that are applied to the dog's skin for absorption into the blood, or given orally, so that the flea dies when it sucks the blood. It is extremely important for you to be aware of which chemicals in your arsenal are cholinesterase inhibitors. Using a yard spray in conjunction with systemics, or some sprays and dips, or with certain worm medications that are also cholinesterase inhibitors, can be a deadly combination.

Insect growth regulators (IGRs) prevent immature fleas from maturing and have proven to be the most highly effective method for long-term flea control. Precor is the most widely used for indoor applications, but is quickly broken down by ultraviolet light. Fenoxicarb is better for outdoor use because it is resistant to ultraviolet light. IGRs are nontoxic to mammals but tend to be expensive. A different type of IGR are nematodes that eat flea larva. Studies show them to be effective and safe, but they must be reapplied regularly since they die when their food supply (the current crop of flea larva) is gone. Newest on the market is lufenuron, an IGR given to the dog orally once a month. Fleas feeding on the dog are sterilized, and lufenuron is extremely safe.

One final warning. There is a popular product on the market that contains "deet" (diethyl-m-toluamide—the same chemical found in some human insect repellants). It has been implicated in the death of many dogs, and is not recommended for Pekes.

Most Pekes are cooperative about nail care as long as they have become accustomed to it from puppyhood.

The Flea Comb

The safest flea control product is the flea comb, a comb with such finely spaced teeth that it catches fleas between them. A flea comb is no match for a fully-coated Peke, however, so is only advisable on clipped or very short-coated dogs. Have a cup of alcohol handy for disposing of the fleas. A cotton ball soaked in alcohol and applied to a flea on the dog will also result in the flea's demise.

Around the House

Because only about 1 to 10 percent of your home's flea population is actually on your dog, you must concentrate on treating your home and yard. These are best treated with a combination adult flea killer and IGR. Cut grass short. Wash all pet bedding and vacuum other surfaces regularly, and especially before applying insecticides. Be sure that sprays reach into small crevices.

Ticks

In some areas, ticks are a greater problem than fleas. Ticks can carry

Grasp a tick as close to its head as possible, and pull with a steady, straight motion toward the rear of the tick.

Rocky Mountain spotted fever, Lyme disease, and most commonly, "tick fever" (erlichiosis), all potentially fatal diseases. They most often burrow in around the ears, head, neck, and feet. Use a tissue

Cut the nails as close to the "quick" as possible.

or tweezers to remove ticks, since some diseases can be transmitted to humans. Grasp the tick as close to the skin as possible, and pull slowly and steadily, trying not to leave the head in the dog. Often a bump will remain after the tick is removed, even if you got the head. It will go away with time. Ticks are so difficult to spot in a Peke's coat that it is best to avoid the woods during tick season.

The Hidden Bear Claws

The long hair of the feet may hide the toenails, causing many owners to neglect cutting the nails as often as needed. When you can hear the pitter-patter of clicking nails, that means that with every step the nails are hitting the floor, and when this happens, the bones of the foot are spread, causing discomfort and eventually splayed feet and lameness. If dewclaws are left untrimmed, they can get caught on things more easily or actually loop around and grow into the dog's leg. You must prevent this by trimming your dog's nails every week or two.

Begin by handling the feet and nails daily, and then cutting the very tips of your puppy's nails every week, taking special care not to cut the "quick" (the central core of blood vessels and nerve endings). You may find it easiest to cut the nails with your Pekingese lying on its back in your lap. If you look at the bottoms of the nails, you will see a solid core culminating in a hollowed nail. Cut the tip up to the core, but not beyond. On occasion, you will slip up and cause the nail to bleed. This is best stopped by styptic powder, but if this is not available, dip the nail in flour or hold it to a wet tea bag.

Keeping the Bite as Bad as the Bark

Pekes have a tendency to lose teeth at an early age, but you can do your best to delay such losses by good dental care.

Between four and seven months of age, Peke puppies will begin to shed their baby teeth and show off new permanent teeth. Often, deciduous (baby) teeth, especially the canines (fangs), are not shed, so that the permanent tooth grows in beside the baby tooth. If this condition persists for over a week, consult your veterinarian. Retained baby teeth can cause misalignment of adult teeth, and are of special concern in toy and brachycephalic breeds, such as the Pekingese.

Correct occlusion is important for good dental health. In a correct Peke bite, the top incisors should be behind the bottom incisors. This prognathic (undershot) bite is common to brachycephalic breeds. Too large a gap between the upper and lower incisors could cause eating difficulties or result in the tongue lolling out of the mouth. Check for rotated teeth, seen most often in the upper jaw of brachycephalic breeds. Such teeth are more prone to increased plaque formation, and may need to be removed for the sake of oral hygiene.

Pekingese can have a problem with plaque and tartar accumulation, which worsens with increasing age. Dry food, hard dog biscuits, and rawhide chewies are helpful, but not totally effective, at removing plaque. Brushing your Peke's teeth once or twice weekly (optimally, daily) with a child's toothbrush and doggy toothpaste is the best plaque remover. If not removed, plaque will attract bacteria and minerals, that will harden into tartar. If you cannot brush, your veterinarian can supply a cleansing solution that will help to kill plaque-forming bacteria, as well as bad breath! You may have to have your veterinarian clean your dog's teeth as often as once a year.

Neglected plaque and tartar can cause infections to form along the gum line. The infection can gradually work its way down the sides of the tooth

Brushing your Peke's teeth is one of the most important health care steps you can take. Left unattended, teeth will accumulate tartar and can become infected and loose. Bottom inset: a healthy tooth. Top inset: an infected tooth.

until the entire root is undermined. The tissues and bone around the tooth erode, and the tooth finally falls out. Meanwhile, the bacteria may have entered the bloodstream and been carried throughout the body, causing infection in the kidneys and heart valves. Neglecting your dog's teeth can do more harm than causing bad breath—it could possibly kill your dog.

Ear Care

The dog's ear canal is made up of an initial long vertical segment that then abruptly angles to run horizontally toward the skull. This configuration, along with hanging hairy ear flaps, provides a moist environment in which various ear infections can flourish. Signs of ear problems include inflammation, discharge, foul odor, pain, scratching, shaking, tilting of the head, or circling to one side. Extreme pain

Healthy eyes are bright, clear, and without tearing.

Never use cotton swabs in the ear canal, as they can irritate the skin and pack debris into the horizontal canal. Never use powders in the ear, which can cake, or hydrogen peroxide, which leaves the ear moist. A Peke with ear problems can benefit from having its ears tied up over its head for a few hours each day to aerate and dry the canals.

Ear Mites: Highly contagious and intensely irritating, ear mites are often found in puppies. Affected dogs will shake their head, scratch their ears, and carry their head sideways. A dark, dry, waxy buildup in the ear canal, usually of both ears, is the ear mite's signature. If you place some of this wax on a piece of dark paper, and have very sharp eyes, you may be able to see the tiny white moving culprits. Over-the-counter ear mite preparations can cause worse irritation, so ear mites should be treated by your veterinarian. Separate a dog with ear mites from other pets and wash your hands after handling its ears.

may indicate a ruptured eardrum. Ear problems can be difficult to cure once they have become established, so early veterinary attention is crucial. Bacterial and fungal infections, ear mites or ticks, foreign bodies, inhalant allergies, seborrhea, or hypothyroidism are possible underlying problems.

The Eyes Have It

The Pekingese eye is subject to more problems than that of most breeds. Special care must be taken to prevent corneal abrasions. Even the Peke's own hair can be an irritant, and long hair should never be allowed to hang over its eyes. The hair of the over-nose wrinkle can grow into the eye unless it is trained daily by pressing the hair of the wrinkle together, or by very carefully snipping it shorter with blunt-nosed scissors.

Corneal abrasions are more common in dogs with bulging eyes, and Pekes from today's better breeders have less bulgy eyes than do typical poorly bred Pekes. But in any Peke, corneal abrasions can occur from scratching the eye with the dog's own paw, yet another reason to get rid of fleas.

Blinking, tearing, or an aversion to bright light are all signs of potential

Good hygiene is as important for a puppy as it is for an adult.

disaster. Examine the cornea (the clear outer surface of the eye) for minute indentations, scratches, or discolored areas that are the early signs of corneal ulcerations. If an ulceration is neglected, the entire cornea can turn whitish in a very short time, and permanent scarring of the cornea can occur even after the eye heals. Pigment granules can appear in the scarred areas and proliferate. In a condition called *pannus*, the cornea becomes progressively covered with pigment or blood vessels, sometimes to the point that the dog becomes completely blind.

Treatment of corneal ulcerations should be under a veterinarian's supervision. As a first step, you can flood the eye with sterile saline solution (such as that available for contact lens wearers) and apply an ophthalmic ointment. Keep the dog out of bright light and prevent it from pawing its eye. An Elizabethan collar is available from your veterinarian that will prevent your dog from reaching its head with its feet. If your dog has dewclaws, you can wrap self-clinging tape (such as Vet-Wrap) around the dog's wrist.

Sustained tearing of the eye could be due to eyelid anomalies that irritate the cornea; if ignored, they could injure the eye to the point of causing blindness. Examine your Peke's eye with a magnifying glass to see if any lashes or hairs from the over-nose wrinkle are turned inward toward the eye (trichiasis), or if there is an abnormal row of lashes (distichiasis—most often on the outer half of the upper lid), or if there is a hair growing from the caruncle, or if the lid itself turns in into the eye (entropion—most often in the middle of the lower lid). These are all serious conditions that may require surgery to prevent extreme discomfort and possible blindness.

A watery discharge can be a symptom of a foreign body, allergies,

The result of consistent and good hygienic care is a dog that is as magnificent to look at as it is fun to play with.

or a tear drainage problem. If accompanied by squinting or pawing, suspect a foreign body in the eye. Examine under the lids and flood the eye with saline solution, or use a moist cotton swab to remove any debris. A clogged tear drainage duct can cause the tears to drain into the face, rather than the normal drainage through the nose. In some Pekingese, the duct may be abnormally small or not present at all. Your veterinarian can diagnose a drainage problem with a simple test.

KCS: A thick ropey mucous or crusty discharge suggests conjunctivitis or dry eye (keratoconjunctivitis sicca, or KCS). In KCS there is inadequate tear production, resulting in irritation to the surface of the eye whenever the dog blinks. The surface of the eye may appear dull. KCS can cause secondary bacterial infection or corneal ulcers. In fact, KCS should be suspected in any dog in which recurrent corneal ulceration or conjunctivitis is a problem. In past years, treatment of KCS was with the frequent application of artificial tears, which most owners found difficult to perform as often as needed. Recent drug advances treat the causes of KCS with ophthalmic immunosuppressive therapy. This therapy can be quite effective if begun early enough, but if you wait until the deeper layers of the cornea are affected, there may be irreversible damage. Therefore, it is imperative that you seek veterinary attention when your Peke has symptoms of KCS.

Lens Problems: As your Peke ages, it is natural that the lens of the eye becomes a little hazy. You will notice this as a slightly grayish appearance behind the pupils. But if this occurs at a young age, or if the lens looks white or opaque, ask your veterinarian to check your Peke for cataracts. In cataracts, the lens becomes so opaque that light can no longer reach the retina; as in humans, the lens can be surgically replaced with an artificial lens.

PRA: The lens focuses light onto the retina of the eye, which is the layer of light sensitive nerve cells. In a hereditary condition known as progressive retinal atrophy (PRA), some of these nerve cells begin to degenerate. At first, the dog seems to have difficulty seeing in dim light; eventually, the dog will become totally blind. There is no cure for PRA, but blind Pekingese can get along just fine as long as you don't rearrange your furniture too often. PRA, while present in the breed, is not widespread.

Prolapse: Because of the Peke's relatively large eyes and shallow eye sockets, it is entirely possible for prolapse of the eye to occur, in which the eyeball actually pops out of the socket in response to a blow to the head. This is obviously an emergency that requires immediate veterinary attention if there is to be any hope of saving the dog's vision. Sometimes the eye will slide back if you pull the lids wide apart, but the more you handle the lids and eye, the more the area will swell, and the more you risk injuring the eye. If it doesn't work with the first try, cover the globe with a moist sponge and get to the veterinarian. The dog may have to be sedated to replace the eye. Sometimes the eye is so injured that sight is never regained; occasionally, the eye itself must be removed. The faster treatment is obtained, the better the chance of recovery.

Any time your dog's pupils do not react to light, or when one eye reacts differently from another, take it to the veterinarian immediately. It could indicate a serious ocular or neurological problem.

In Sickness and in Health

Your dog can tell you where it hurts if you only know how to listen to it—by means of a weekly health check and a regular veterinary checkup.

The Health Check

A weekly health check should be part of your grooming procedure. The health check should include examining the eyes for discharge or cloudiness, irregular or dark surface, or red or yellow "whites" of the eye; the ears for bad smell, redness, or discharge; the mouth for red, bleeding, or swollen gums, loose teeth, ulcers of the tongue or gums, or bad breath; the nose for thickened or colored discharge; the skin for parasites, hair loss, crusts, red spots, or lumps. Many bumps and lumps are not cause for concern, but because there is always a possibility of cancer, they should be examined by your veterinarian. This is especially true of a sore that does not heal, or any pigmented lump that begins to grow or bleed.

Observe your dog for signs of lameness or incoordination, a sore neck, circling, loss of muscling, and for any behavioral change. Run your hands over the muscles and bones and check that they are symmetrical from one side to the other. Check the toes, nails, and pads. Weigh your dog and observe whether it is putting on fat or wasting away. Look out for mammary masses, changes in testicle size, discharge from the vulva or penis, increased or decreased urination, foul-smelling or strangely colored urine,

incontinence, swollen abdomen, black or bloody stool, change in appetite or water consumption, difficulty breathing, lethargy, gagging, or loss of balance.

Doggy odor is not only offensive; it is unnatural. Don't exile the dog, or hold your breath. If a bath doesn't produce results, it's time to smell your reeking Peking dog. Use your nose to pinpoint the source of the problem. Infection is a common cause of bad odor; check the over-nose wrinkle, the gums, the ears, the feet, and the genitals. Generalized bad odor can indicate a skin problem, such as

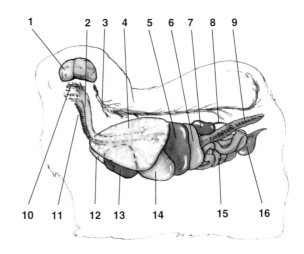

Internal organs of the Pekingese. 1. Brain, 2. Esophagus, 3. Spinal cord, 4. Lungs, 5. Stomach, 6. Spleen, 7. Kidney, 8. Ureter, 9. Descending colon, 10. Sinus cavity, 11. Trachea, 12. Thymus, 13. Heart, 14. Liver, 15. Intestine, 16. Bladder

Only with good health care can your Pekingese live a long, active life.

Preventive Medicine

The best preventive medicine is that which prevents accidents: a well-trained dog in a well-fenced yard or on a leash, and a properly Peke-proofed home. Other preventive steps must be taken to avoid diseases and parasites, however.

Vaccinations

Rabies, distemper, leptospirosis, canine hepatitis, parvovirus, and corona-virus are highly contagious and deadly diseases that have broken many a loving owner's heart in the past. Now that vaccinations are available for these maladies, one would think they would no longer be a threat, but many dogs remain unvaccinated and continue to succumb to and spread these potentially fatal illnesses. Don't let your Pekingese be one of them.

Vaccinations are also available for kennel cough and Lyme disease, but may be optional, depending upon your dog's life style. Your veterinarian can advise you. Always make sure your dog is in good health at the time it is

seborrhea (see page 60). Don't ignore bad odor, and don't make your dog take the blame for something you need to fix.

Choosing Your Veterinarian

When choosing your veterinarian, consider availability, emergency arrangements, costs, facilities, and ability to communicate. You and your veterinarian will form a partnership that will work together to protect your Peke's health, so your rapport with your veterinarian is very important. Your veterinarian should listen to your observations, and should explain to you exactly what is happening with your pet. The clinic should be clean, and have safe, sanitary overnight accommodations. After-hour emergency arrangements should be made clear.

When you take your dog to the veterinary clinic, hold your dog on your lap or in a cage. If you think your dog may have a contagious illness, inform the clinic beforehand so that you can use another entrance. Your veterinarian will be appreciative if your Pekingese is clean and under control during the examination. Warn your veterinarian if you think there is any chance that your dog may bite.

An ounce of prevention...

Sample Vaccination Schedule

Age (weeks)	Vaccine
6–8	distemper + hepatitis + parainfluenza + parvovirus
10–12	distemper + hepatitis + parainfluenza + parvovirus + leptospirosis
14–16	distemper + hepatitis + parainfluenza + parvovirus + leptospirosis, rabies
18–20	distemper + hepatitis + parainfluenza + parvovirus + leptospirosis

vaccinated. Many dogs seem to feel under the weather for a day or so after getting their vaccinations, so don't schedule your appointment the day before boarding, a trip, or a big doggy event.

Puppies receive their dam's immunity through nursing in the first days of life. This is why it is important that your pup's mother be properly immunized before breeding, and that your pup be able to nurse from its dam. The immunity gained from the mother will wear off after several weeks, and then the pup will be susceptible to disease unless you provide immunity through vaccinations. The problem is that there is no way to know exactly when this passive immunity will wear off, and vaccinations given before that time are ineffective. So you must revaccinate over a period of weeks so that your pup will not be unprotected and will receive lasting immunity. Your pup's breeder will have given the first vaccinations to your pup before it was old enough to go home with you. Bring all information about your pup's vaccination history to your veterinarian on your first visit so that the pup's vaccination schedule can be maintained. Meanwhile, it is best not to let your pup mingle with strange dogs.

Internal Parasite Control

Heartworms: Heartworms are a deadly nematode parasite carried by mosquitos. Wherever mosquitoes are present, dogs should be on heartworm prevention. Several effective types of heartworm preventive are available, with some also preventing many other types of worms. Even though the Peke's abundant coat provides it with some protection, a mosquito can still bite it on the face. Ask your veterinarian when your puppy should begin taking the preventive. If you forget to give it as

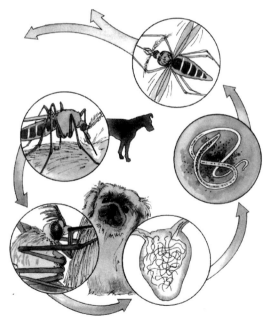

Life-cycle of heartworms. When a mosquito bites an infected dog, it ingests circulating immature heartworms, which it then passes on to the next dog it bites.

The life-cycle of the tapeworm. Note that a flea is a necessary intermediate host.

until hormonal changes due to her pregnancy cause them to be activated, and then they infect her fetuses or her newborns through her milk.

You may be tempted to pick up some worm medication and worm your puppy yourself. Don't. Over-the-counter wormers are largely ineffective and often more dangerous than those available through your veterinarian. Left untreated, worms can cause vomiting, diarrhea, dull coat, listlessness, anemia, and death. Have your puppy tested for internal parasites regularly. Some heartworm preventatives also prevent most types of intestinal worms (but not tapeworms).

Tapeworms (cestodes) tend to plague some dogs throughout their lives. There is no preventive, except to diligently rid your Pekingese of fleas, because fleas transmit tapeworms to dogs. Tapeworms look like moving white worms on fresh stools, or may dry up and look like rice grains around the dog's anus. Tapeworms are one of the least harmful worms, but their segments can be irritating to the dog's anal region, and are certainly unsightly.

Common Misconceptions about Worms
• Misconception: A dog that is scooting its rear along the ground has worms. Although this may be a sign of tapeworms, a dog that repeatedly scoots more likely has impacted anal sacs.
• Misconception: Feeding a dog sugar and sweets will give it worms. There are good reasons not to feed a dog sweets, but worms have nothing to do with them.
• Misconception: Dogs should be regularly wormed every month or so. Dogs should be wormed when, and only when, they have been diagnosed with worms. No worm medication is completely without risk, and it is foolish to use it carelessly.

prescribed, your Peke may get heartworms. A dog with suspected heartworms should not be given the preventive because a fatal reaction could occur. Heartworms are treatable in their early stages, but the treatment is expensive and not without risks. If untreated, heartworms can kill your pet.

Intestinal parasites: Hookworms, whipworms, ascarids, threadworms, and lungworms are all types of nematode parasites that can infect dogs of all ages, but have their most devastating effect on puppies. When you take the pup to be vaccinated, bring along a stool specimen so that your veterinarian can also check for these parasites. Most puppies do have worms at some point, even pups from the most fastidious breeders. This is because some types of larval worms become encysted in the dam's body long before she ever became pregnant, perhaps when she herself was a pup. Here they lie dormant and immune from worming,

Protozoa: Puppies and dogs also suffer from protozoan parasites, such as coccidia and especially, *Giardia.* These can cause chronic or intermittent diarrhea, and can be diagnosed with a stool specimen.

Common Ailments and Symptoms

Problems of the hair and skin are described on pages 59–60; those of the teeth, ears, and eyes on pages 62–66.

Diarrhea: All dogs get diarrhea, but in Pekingese it is not only a health concern, but a potential grooming nightmare. Diarrhea can result from overexcitement or nervousness, a change in diet or water, sensitivity to certain foods, overeating, intestinal parasites, viral or bacterial infections, or ingestion of toxic substances. Bloody diarrhea, diarrhea with vomiting, fever, or other signs of toxicity, or diarrhea that lasts for more than a day should not be allowed to continue without veterinary advice. Some of these could be symptomatic of potentially fatal disorders.

Less severe diarrhea can be treated at home by withholding or severely restricting food and water for 24 hours. Ice cubes can be given to satisfy thirst. Administer Immodium in the same weight dosage as recommended for humans. A bland diet consisting of rice, tapioca, or cooked macaroni, along with cottage cheese or tofu for protein, should be given for several days. Feed nothing else. The intestinal tract needs time off in order to heal.

Vomiting: Vomiting is a common occurrence that may or may not indicate a serious problem. You should consult your veterinarian immediately if your dog vomits a foul substance resembling fecal matter (indicating a blockage in the intestinal tract), blood (partially digested blood resembles coffee grounds), or if there is projectile vomiting. Sporadic vomiting with poor appetite and generally poor condition could indicate internal parasites or a more serious internal disease that should also be checked by your veterinarian.

Overeating is a common cause of occasional vomiting in puppies, especially if they follow eating with playing. Feed smaller meals more frequently if this becomes a problem. Vomiting after eating grass is common and usually of no great concern. Vomiting immediately after meals could indicate an obstruction of the esophagus. Repeated vomiting could indicate that the dog has eaten spoiled food, undigestible objects, or may have a stomach illness. Veterinary advice should be sought. Meanwhile, withhold food (or feed as directed for diarrhea), and restrict water.

Coughing: Any persistent cough should be checked by your veterinarian. Coughing irritates the throat and can lead to secondary infections if allowed to continue unchecked. It can also cause swelling of the larynx, possibly interfering with breathing. There are many reasons for coughing, including allergies, foreign bodies, pneumonia, tracheal collapse, and tumors, but two of the most common are kennel cough and heart disease.

Kennel cough is a highly communicable airborne disease caused by several different infectious agents, but all cause similar symptoms. Vaccinations are available and are an especially good idea if you plan to have your dog around other dogs at training classes or while being boarded.

Heart disease can result in coughing following exercise or in the evening. Treatment with diuretics and specific heart medication(s) prescribed by your veterinarian can help alleviate the coughing for a while.

Urinary tract diseases: If your dog has difficulty or pain in urination, uri-

The Pekingese typically lives a long life.

some simple tests, and each of these conditions can be treated. For kidney disease, a low-protein and low-sodium diet can slow the progression.

In males, infections of the prostate gland can lead to repeated urinary tract infections, and sometimes painful defecation or blood and pus in the urine. Long-term antibiotic therapy and castration is required for improvement.

Pekingese are prone to uroliths (kidney and urinary bladder stones), which can be especially serious in male dogs. Urinary incontinence is often seen in spayed females, and can be treated with drugs. Incontinence can also be due to intervertebral disc rupture, and may be improved with surgery.

Impacted anal sacs: Dogs have two anal sacs that are normally emptied by rectal pressure during defecation. Their musky smelling contents may also be forcibly ejected when a dog is extremely frightened. Sometimes they fail to empty properly and become impacted or infected. This is more common in small dogs, obese dogs, dogs with seborrhea, and dogs that seldom have firm stools. Constant licking of the anus or scooting of the anus along the ground are characteristic signs of anal sac impaction. Not only is this an extremely uncomfortable condition for your dog, but left unattended, the impacted sacs can become infected. Your veterinarian can show you how to empty the anal sacs yourself. Some dogs may never need to have their anal sacs expressed, but others may need regular attention. In some instances, these sacs may require surgical removal.

Endocrine disorders: Hormone-related disorders in the dog include diabetes, hypothyroidism, and Cushing's syndrome. The most common is hypothyroidism; its signs are often subtle, but may include weight gain, lethargy, and coat problems such

nates suddenly and often, but in small amounts, or passes cloudy or bloody urine, it may be suffering from a problem of the bladder, urethra, or prostate. Your veterinarian will need to examine your Pekingese to determine the exact nature of the problem. Bladder infections must be treated promptly to prevent the infection from reaching the kidneys.

Kidney disease, ultimately leading to kidney failure, is one of the most common ailments of older dogs. The earliest symptom is usually increased urination. Although the excessive urination may cause problems in keeping your house clean or your night's sleep intact, *never* try to restrict water from a dog with kidney disease. Increased urination can also be a sign of diabetes or a urinary tract infection. Your veterinarian can determine the cause with as oiliness, dullness, **symmetrical** hair loss, and hair that is easily pulled out.

The symptoms of diabetes include increased drinking and urination, and sometimes increased appetite with weight loss.

Cushing's syndrome (hyperadrenocorticism) is seen mostly in older dogs, and is characterized by increased drinking and urination, a pot-bellied appearance, symmetrical hair loss on the body, and hyperpigmentation of the skin. This condition is often accompanied by infections because Cushing's dogs have diminished immunity to infection.

All of these conditions can be diagnosed with simple tests, and can be effectively treated with drugs.

Limping: Puppies are especially susceptible to bone and joint injuries, and should never be allowed to jump from high places or run until exhausted. Persistent limping in puppies may result from one of several developmental bone problems, and should be professionally evaluated. Both puppies and adults should be kept off slippery floors that could cause them to lose their footing. Clipping the long hair that covers the foot pads can also help prevent your Peke from slipping.

Limping may or may not indicate a serious problem. When associated with extreme pain, fever, swelling, deformity, or grinding or popping sounds, you should have your veterinarian examine your Pekingese at once. Ice packs may help minimize swelling if applied immediately after an injury. Fractures should be immobilized by splinting above and below the site of fracture (small rolled magazines work well on legs) before moving the dog. Mild lameness should be treated by complete rest; if it still persists after three days, your dog will need to be examined by its veterinarian.

Knee injuries are common in dogs; most do not get well on their own. Avoid pain medications that might encourage the use of an injured limb.

In older dogs, or dogs with a previous injury, limping is often the result of osteoarthritis. Arthritis can be treated with aspirin, but should be done so only under veterinary supervision. Do not use ibuprofen or naxopren.

Toy breeds are more prone to rheumatoid arthritis. Any time a young or middle-aged dog shows signs of arthritis, especially in a joint that has not been previously injured, it should be examined by its veterinarian.

Many small breeds, including (to some extent) Pekingese, are prone to patellar luxation (displaced kneecap), especially when they are young. In most dogs, the patella is held in its proper position by a deep groove, but in some Pekes the groove is too shallow. In these dogs, you can actually push the patella out of place to either the inside or outside of the knee. When out of place, the dog cannot straighten its leg, and will tend to hold the affected

To reach its full potential, good care should start when your Peke is a puppy.

73

The Medical Kit

You should maintain a first aid/medical kit for your Pekingese, which should contain at least:

- rectal thermometer
- scissors
- tweezer
- sterile gauze dressings
- self-adhesive bandage
- instant cold compress
- antidiarrhea medication
- ophthalmic ointment
- soap
- antiseptic skin ointment
- hydrogen peroxide
- clean sponge
- pen light
- syringe
- towel
- stethoscope (optional)
- oxygen (optional)
- first aid instructions
- veterinarian and emergency clinic numbers
- poison control center number

leg up for several steps until the patella pops back into place. While standing, it may appear either knock-kneed or bow-legged. This condition can be surgically repaired. If it is present in a puppy, the repair should be done by a few months of age, before the leg becomes permanently deformed.

Lameness in which the leg appears paralyzed, or when the dog places the top of the foot on the ground, could be due to nerve damage. One of the more common types of rear end paralysis in Pekes results from herniated intervertebral discs, which may or may not respond to surgical treatment. The possibility of herniated discs can be lessened by not allowing your Peke to jump off furniture or high places.

Medications

Don't give your dog human medications unless you have been directed to do so by your veterinarian. Some medications for humans have no effect on dogs, and some can have a very detrimental effect. When giving pills, open your dog's mouth and place the pill well to the back and in the middle of the tongue. Close the mouth and gently stroke the throat until your dog swallows. Pre-wetting capsules or covering them with cream cheese or some other food helps prevent capsules from sticking to the tongue or roof of the mouth. For liquid medicine, tilt the head back and place the liquid in the pouch of the cheek. Then close your dog's mouth until it swallows. Always give the full course of medications prescribed by your veterinarian.

On occasion, you may also need to take your dog's temperature. Use a rectal thermometer, preferably the digital type, lubricate it, and insert it about 1.5 inches (3.8 cm). Do not allow your dog to sit down because the thermometer could break. Normal temperature for a small dog is around 102°F (38.9°C). Incidentally, not only do small dogs tend to have a slightly higher body temperature than do large dogs, but they also tend to have a higher heart rate, averaging about 180 beats per minute (200 to 220 per minute for puppies). A good place to check the pulse is on the femoral artery, located inside the rear leg, where the thigh meets the abdomen.

The Pekingese Pensioner

When is a Pekingese geriatric? It varies between dogs, but most small dogs are described as geriatric at 10 to 12 years of age. In a 1960 study of 158 Pekingese, 80 percent of Pekes that reached adulthood lived to be at least five years of age, 62 percent were alive at 10 years, 36 percent reached their fourteenth year, but none of these survived another year.

As your Peke ages, you may first notice that it sleeps longer and more soundly than it did as a youngster.

Upon awakening, it is slower to get going and may be stiff at first. It may be less eager to play and more content to lie in the sun. Some dogs become cranky and less patient, especially when dealing with puppies or boisterous children. But don't just excuse behavioral changes, especially if sudden, as due simply to aging. They could be symptoms of pain or disease.

Older dogs may seem to ignore their owner's commands, but this may be the result of hearing loss. Take care not to startle a dog with impaired hearing, as a startled dog could snap in self-defense. The slight haziness that appears in the older dog's pupils is normal and has minimal effect upon vision, but some dogs, especially those with diabetes, may develop cataracts. These can be removed by a veterinary ophthalmologist if they are severe. Decreased tear production increases the chances of KCS (dry eye) in older Pekes (see page 65). Dogs with gradual vision loss can cope well as long as they are kept in familiar surroundings. Don't rearrange furniture, close usually open doors, or come upon a blind Peke without first speaking. Use baby gates at the head of stairs or edges of decks.

Arthritis is a common cause of intermittent lameness. A soft warm bed combined with moderate activity can help, and your veterinarian can prescribe drugs for severe cases.

In some Pekes, the intervertebral discs gradually become displaced and exert pressure on the spinal cord, causing paralysis of the hind legs. Surgery is not always successful, and the dog may need special care for the rest of its life. Carts are available that cradle the dog's pelvis and enable the dog to roll merrily along.

Paralysis is one of several causes for loss of bowel and bladder control. If your veterinarian can find no medical reason, use plastic sheeting or doggy diapers.

Feeding the Older Dog

Both physical activity and metabolic rates decrease in older animals, meaning that they require fewer calories to maintain the same weight. It is important to keep your older dog active. Older dogs that continue to be fed the same amount as when they were young risk becoming obese; such dogs have a greater risk of cardiovascular and joint problems.

Older dogs should be fed several small meals instead of one large meal, and should be fed on time. Moistening dry food or feeding canned food can help a dog with tooth loss enjoy its meal.

Unless a dog has been diagnosed with kidney disease, there is no reason to switch to a low-protein diet. Although many geriatric dogs are overweight, others lose weight and may need to eat puppy food in order to keep the pounds on. There are a variety of reduced calorie, low-protein senior diets on the market. But most older dogs do not require a special diet unless they have a particular medical need for it (e.g., obesity: low calorie; kidney failure: low protein; heart failure: low sodium). Dogs with these problems may require special prescription dog foods that better address their needs.

Skin Care

Like people, dogs lose skin moisture as they age, and though dogs don't wrinkle, their skin can become dry and itchy as a result. Regular brushing can stimulate oil production. Older dogs tend to have a stronger body odor, but don't just ignore increased odors. They could indicate specific problems, such as periodontal disease, impacted anal sacs, seborrhea, ear infections, or even kidney disease. Any strong odor should be checked by your veterinarian.

Health Risks

There is evidence that the immune system may be less effective in older

Your Pekingese will look to, and depend on, you for all its health needs. Don't let it down!

dogs. This means that it is increasingly important to shield your dog from infectious disease, chilling, overheating, and any stressful conditions. Older dogs present a somewhat greater anesthesia risk. Most of this increased risk can be negated, however, by first screening dogs with a complete medical workup.

Long trips may be grueling, and boarding in a kennel may be extremely upsetting. Introduction of a puppy or new pet may be welcomed and encourage your older dog to play, but if your dog is not used to other dogs, the newcomer will more likely be resented and be an additional source of stress.

The older dog should be seen by its veterinarian at least biyearly. Blood tests can detect early stages of disease that can benefit from treatment. The owner must take responsibility for observing any health changes. Some of the more common changes, along with some of the more common conditions they may indicate in older dogs, are:
• Limping: arthritis, patellar luxation
• Nasal discharge: tumor, periodontal disease

• Coughing: heart disease, tracheal collapse, lung cancer
• Difficulty eating: periodontal disease, oral tumors
• Decreased appetite: kidney, liver, or heart disease, pancreatitis, cancer
• Increased appetite: diabetes, Cushing's syndrome
• Weight loss: heart, liver or kidney disease, diabetes, cancer
• Abdominal distension: heart or kidney disease, Cushing's syndrome, tumor
• Increased urination: diabetes, kidney, or liver disease, cystitis, Cushing's syndrome
• Diarrhea: kidney or liver disease, pancreatitis

The above list is by no means inclusive of all symptoms or problems they may indicate. Vomiting and diarrhea can signal many different problems; keep in mind that a small older dog cannot tolerate the dehydration that results from continued vomiting or diarrhea and you should not let it continue unchecked.

In general, any ailment that an older dog has is magnified in severity compared to the same symptoms in a younger dog. This is especially true of any problems with breathing or overheating in the Peke. Don't be lulled into a false sense of security just because you own a Pekingese. A long life depends upon good genes, good care, and good luck.

If you are lucky enough to have an old Pekingese, you still must accept that an end will come. Heart disease, kidney failure, and cancer eventually claim most of these senior citizens. Early detection can help delay their effects, but unfortunately, can seldom prevent them ultimately.

Till Death Do Us Part

Unfortunately there comes the time when, no matter how diligent you have been, neither you nor your veterinarian can prevent your cherished pet from succumbing to old age or an incurable illness. It seems hard to believe that you will have to say good-bye to someone who has been such a focal point of your life, in truth, a real member of your family. That dogs live such a short time compared to humans is a cruel fact, and as much as you may wish otherwise, your Pekingese is a dog and is not immortal.

You should realize that both of you have been fortunate to have shared so many good times, but make sure that your Peke's remaining time is still pleasurable. Many terminal illnesses make your dog feel very sick indeed, and there comes a point where your desire to keep your friend with you as long as possible may not be the kindest thing for either of you. If your Peke no longer eats its dinner or treats, this is a sign that it does not feel well, and you must face the prospect of doing what is best for your beloved friend.

Euthanasia is a difficult and personal decision that no one wishes to make, but no one can make for you. Ask your veterinarian if there is a reasonable chance of your dog getting better, and if it is likely your dog is suffering. Ask yourself if your dog is getting pleasure out of life, and if it enjoys most of its days. Financial considerations can be a factor if it means going into debt in exchange for just a little while longer. Your own emotional state must also be considered.

If you do decide that euthanasia is the kindest farewell gift for your beloved friend, discuss with your veterinarian beforehand what will happen. Euthanasia is painless and involves giving an overdose of an anesthetic. If your dog is scared of the veterinarian's office, you might feel better having the doctor meet you at home or come out to your car. Although it won't be easy, try to remain with your Pekingese so that its last moments will be filled with your love; otherwise, have a friend that your dog knows stay with it. Try to recall the wonderful times you have shared and realize that however painful losing such a once-in-a-lifetime dog is, it is better than never having had such a friend in the first place.

Many people who regarded their pet as a member of the family nonetheless feel embarrassed at the grief they feel at its loss. Yet this dog has often functioned as a surrogate child, best friend, and confidant. We should all be lucky enough to find a human with the faithful and loving qualities of our dogs. In some ways, the loss of a pet can be harder than that of more distant family members, especially because the support from friends that comes with human loss is too often absent with pet loss. Such well-meaning but ill-informed statements as "he was just a dog" or "just get another one" do little to ease the pain, but the truth is that many people simply don't know how to react and probably aren't really as callous as they might sound. There are, however, many people who share your feelings and there are pet bereavement counselors available at many veterinary schools.

After losing a dog, many people say they will never get another. True, no dog will ever take the place of your dog. But you will find that another dog is a welcome diversion and will help keep you from dwelling on the loss of your first pet, as long as you don't keep comparing the new dog to the old. It is also true that by getting another dog you are sentencing yourself to the same grief in another 10 to 15 years, but wouldn't you rather have that than miss out on all of the love and companionship altogether?

HOW-TO:
Dealing With Emergencies

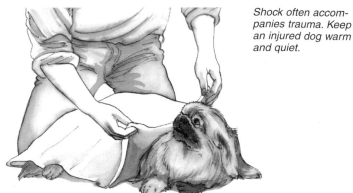

Shock often accompanies trauma. Keep an injured dog warm and quiet.

Know the phone number and location of the emergency veterinarian in your area. Make sure you always have enough fuel in your car to make it to the emergency clinic without stopping to find a gas station.

Deciding whether or not you have an emergency can sometimes be difficult. What would not be an emergency for the average dog may very well be an emergency for a Peke. The following situations are all emergencies. **For all cases, administer the first aid treatment outlined and seek the nearest veterinary help immediately.** Call the clinic first so that they can prepare.

In General
• Make sure breathing passages are open. Remove any collar and check the mouth and throat.
• Be calm and reassuring. A calm dog is less likely to go into shock.
• Move the dog as little and as gently as possible.
Shock
Signs: Very pale gums, weakness, unresponsiveness, faint pulse, shivering.

Treatment: Keep the dog warm and calm; control any bleeding; check breathing, pulse, and consciousness, and treat these problems if needed.

Heatstroke
Signs: Rapid, loud breathing; abundant thick saliva, bright red mucous membranes, high rectal temperature. Later signs: unsteadiness, diarrhea, coma.

Treatment: Immediately immerse the dog in cool (not ice) water and then place it in front of a fan. You must lower your dog's body temperature quickly (but do not lower it below 100°F [37.8°C]). If your dog has been shaved, it is better to cover it with a cold wet towel and place it in front of a fan.

Breathing Difficulties
Signs: Gasping for breath with head extended, anxiety, weakness; advances to loss of consciousness, blueish tongue (exception: carbon monoxide poisoning causes a bright red tongue).

Treatment: If not breathing, give mouth-to-nose respiration:
1. Open dog's mouth, clear passage of secretions and foreign bodies.
2. Pull dog's tongue forward.
3. Seal your mouth over dog's nose and mouth; blow gently into dog's nose for three seconds, then release.
4. Continue until dog breathes on its own.

If due to **drowning,** turn dog upside down, holding it by the hind legs, so that water can run out of its mouth. Then administer mouth-to-nose respiration, with the dog's head positioned lower than its lungs.

For **obstructions,** wrap your hands around the abdomen, behind the rib cage, and compress briskly. Repeat if needed. If the dog loses consciousness, extend the head and neck forward, pull the tongue out fully, and explore the throat for any foreign objects.

Cessation of Pulse
Signs: No pulse, heartbeat, or breathing.

Treatment: Administer cardiac massage. Place hand on the chest behind the elbow, and depress 1.5 inches (3.8 cm) at a rate of 100 times per minute.

Poisoning
Signs: Varies according to poison, but commonly include vomiting, convulsions, staggering, collapse

Treatment: Call the veterinarian or poison control hotline at once and give as much information as possible. Induce vomiting (except in the cases outlined below) by giving either hydrogen peroxide (mixed 1:1 with water), salt water, or dry mustard and water. Treat for shock and get to the veterinarian immediately. Be prepared for convulsions or respiratory distress.

Do *not* induce vomiting if the poison was an acid, alkali, petroleum product, solvent, cleaner, tranquilizer, or if a sharp object was swallowed; also do *not* induce vomiting if the dog is severely depressed, convulsing, comatose, or if over two hours have passed since ingestion.

If the dog is not convulsing or unconscious: dilute the poison by giving milk, vegetable oil, or egg whites. Activated charcoal can adsorb many toxins. Baking soda or milk of magnesia can be given for ingested acids, and vinegar or lemon juice for ingested alkalis.

Two of the most common and life-threatening poisons eaten by dogs are Warfarin (rodent poison) and ethylene glycol (antifreeze). Veterinary treatment must be obtained within two to four hours of ingestion of even tiny amounts if the dog's life is to be saved.

Convulsions

Signs: Drooling, stiffness, muscle spasms.

Treatment: Wrap the dog securely in a blanket to prevent it from injuring itself on the furniture or stairs. Remove other dogs from the area. *Never* put your hands in a convulsing dog's mouth. Treat for shock. Make note of all characteristics and sequences of seizure activity, which can help to diagnose the cause.

Snakebites

Signs: Swelling, discoloration, pain, fang marks, restlessness, nausea, weakness.

Treatment: Restrain the dog and keep it quiet. Be able to describe the snake. Only if you can't get to the veterinarian, except when the bite is on the head, apply a tourniquet between the bite and the heart, tight enough to prevent blood returning to the heart.

Open Wounds

Signs: Consider wounds to be an emergency if there is profuse bleeding, if extremely deep, or if open to chest cavity, abdominal cavity, or head.

Treatment: Control massive bleeding first. Cover the wound with clean dressing and apply pressure; apply more dressings over the others until bleeding stops. Also elevate wound site, and apply cold pack to site. If an extremity, apply pressure to the closest pressure point as follows:
• For a front leg: inside of front leg just above the elbow
• For a rear leg: inside of the thigh where the femoral artery crosses the thighbone
• For the tail: underside of the tail close to where it joins the body.

Transport to a veterinarian immediately.

Use a tourniquet only in life-threatening situations and when all other attempts have failed. Check for signs of shock.

Sucking chest wounds: Place a sheet of plastic or other nonporous material over the hole and bandage it to make as airtight a seal as possible.

Abdominal wounds: Place a warm wet sterile dressing over any protruding internal organs; cover with a bandage or towel. Do not attempt to push organs back into the dog.

Head wounds: Apply gentle pressure to control bleeding. Monitor for loss of consciousness or shock and treat accordingly.

Deep Burns

Signs: Charred or pearly white skin; deeper layers of tissue exposed.

Treatment: Cool burned area with cool packs, towels soaked in ice water, or by immersing in cold water. If over 50 percent of the dog is burned, do not immerse, as this increases the likelihood of shock. Cover with a clean bandage or towel to avoid contamination. Do not apply pressure; do not apply ointments. Monitor for shock.

Electrical Shock

Signs: Collapse, burns inside mouth.

Treatment: Before touching the dog, disconnect the plug or cut power; if that cannot be done immediately, use a wooden pencil, spoon, or broom handle to knock the cord away from the dog. Keep the dog warm and treat for shock. Monitor breathing and heartbeat.

Again, the procedures outlined above are first aid only. They do not take the place of the emergency veterinary clinic. Nor is the above list a complete catalog of emergency situations. Situations not described can usually be treated with the same first aid as for humans.

Breeding Pekingese of Quality

A Bad Idea

One of the most unfortunate aspects of dog ownership is the compulsion so many people have to breed a litter. Rarely is this done with any foresight or responsibility. The result, most often, is a grave disservice to themselves, their pet, the breed, the resulting puppies, and to their new owners. Unless you have studied the breed, have proven your female to be a superior specimen in terms of conformation, health, and temperament, and plan to take responsibility for each and every puppy for the rest of its life, you have no business doing anything but having your dog neutered. Keep in mind:

• A spayed female is much less likely to develop breast cancer and a number of other hormone-related diseases. She should be spayed before her first season in order to avoid these problems.

• A high percentage of Pekingese require expensive Caesarean sections, and sometimes inexperienced dams won't recognize a pup from a Caesarean section as their responsibility to raise. You may end up bottle-feeding and being a surrogate mom.

• There is definite discomfort and a certain amount of danger to any dog, but especially a Pekingese, when whelping a litter. Watching a litter being born is *not* a good way to teach the children the miracle of life; there are too many things that can go wrong.

• Pekingese litters tend to be small, yet may cost as much to raise as a large litter. Selling a pup will probably not come close to reimbursing you for the stud fee, prenatal care, whelping complications, Caesarean sections, supplemental feeding, puppy food, vaccinations, advertising, and a staggering investment of time and energy.

• Serious breeders have spent years researching genetics and the breed, breed only the best specimens, and screen for hereditary defects in order to obtain superior puppies. Until you have done the same, you are undoing the hard work of those who have dedicated their lives to bettering the breed.

• There are many more purebred Pekingese in the world than there are good homes for them. The puppy you sell to a less-than-perfect buyer may end up neglected or discarded, or used to produce puppies to sell to even less desirable homes. Millions of purebreds are euthanized each year at pounds. Sometimes they are the lucky ones.

• The fact that your Pekingese is purebred and registered does not mean it is breeding quality, any more than the fact that you have a driver's license qualifies you to build race cars. Review the definition of breeding quality given on page 20.

Ethical breeders breed a litter only after studying the breed standard, studying pedigrees, and studying individual dogs to find the most advantageous match of conformation, temperament, and health, then proving the worth of both prospective parents through competitions. They interview prospective buyers and get deposits

Does your Pekingese look like this? If not, don't breed her. Refer to the Pekingese standard and compare your Peke to it with an impartial eye.

from them before the breeding even takes place. They have money set aside for prenatal and postnatal care, and emergency funds and vacation time available for whelping or post-whelping complications. They have the commitment to keep every single puppy born for the rest of its life should good homes not be available or should they ever have to be returned. And they worry a lot. Is it any wonder that some of the best breeders breed the least?

Pekingese Problems

The breeding of dogs is far too often undertaken by people who have no idea about what to do even if everything goes smoothly, much less if things go wrong. And things have a tendency to go very wrong when dealing with Pekingese pregnancies.

Dystocia and Caesarian sections: Brachycephalic breeds, breeds with large forequarters and narrow hindquarters, and small breeds in general have a greater tendency to have *dystocia*, the difficulty or inability to deliver a puppy through the birth canal. Pekingese are prone to dystocia, and often require Caesarean sections (C-sections) to save the lives of the pups and dam. Owners should calculate the expected delivery date so that they can be prepared for a trip to the veterinarian. Leaving a Peke unattended when it might be in whelping distress could be a fatal mistake.

Many experienced Peke breeders elect to have a C-section performed for every litter. In this way the dam is not already in trouble before undergoing surgery, and arrangements can be made for surgery during regular office hours. Scheduled C-sections generally cost about $250 to $300; emergency C-sections can cost around $700.

Eclampsia: Eclampsia is a life-threatening convulsive condition that may occur in late pregnancy or more commonly, during lactation. It is more prevalent in small breeds and with larger litters. The first signs are nervous panting and restlessness, followed by increasing irritability and disorientation. Muscular twitching, fever, and rapid heart rate are definite danger signals. Convulsions are the last stage before death.

The condition is brought about by a depletion of calcium. Many breeders of small dogs used to supplement with calcium throughout the pregnancy in an attempt to ward off eclampsia, but it is now thought that such supplementation may actually promote eclampsia by interfering with the internal calcium-regulating mechanisms.

Once eclampsia does occur, the bitch must be taken immediately to the veterinarian for an injection of calcium and Vitamin D in order to save her life. Calcium may be given by mouth if she can swallow and if the trip to the veterinarian is long, but even then may not be absorbed enough to help much. *Eclampsia is an extreme emergency.*

Breeding the Right Way

If you still have not been dissuaded from breeding your Pekingese, you owe it to yourself and the breed to settle for no less than the best available Pekingese stud. You will not find this stud advertised in the newspaper. If you are contemplating breeding, it is assumed that you have now learned enough about the breed that you are familiar with prominent kennels and studs. Look for a stud that is superior in the areas in which your bitch needs improvement. Look for a stud owner who is honest about his or her dog's faults, health problems, and temperament. A responsible stud owner will have proven the stud by earning titles, will have complete records and photos of other litters the stud has produced, and will insist that your bitch and her pedigree be compatible before accepting her for breeding.

Long before your female comes into season, you should have a written contract with the stud dog owner that spells out what fees will be due and when, and what will happen if no puppies are born. Both dogs to be bred should have a blood test for canine brucellosis, a primarily (but not exclusively) sexually transmitted disease with devastating effects on fertility. The female should also have a prebreeding checkup to ensure that she is in good health, has current vaccinations, and does not have any abnormalities that would make for a difficult pregnancy.

The Royal Courtship

Monitor the female closely for signs of "heat" (estrus). These include swelling of the vulva and a red discharge, but in many Pekes these signs may be subtle and go unnoticed. Most dogs are breedable for several days sometime between the eighth and eighteenth day of estrus, although earlier and later alliances have been known to result in pregnancy. Your veterinarian can also monitor her progress with vaginal smears or blood tests. As she approaches her receptive stage, she will tend to "flag" her tail, or cock it to the side when the male approaches or if you scratch around the base of her tail. Your best indicator is the stud dog; experienced stud dogs do not need calendars or microscopes!

Breeding dogs involves more than just letting a male and female loose together. Although this may seem like the natural way, in fact it is not natural for two dogs to breed when they may have just met each other. Neither dog knows the other well enough to trust its actions, so the female will often snap in fear when the male mounts, and the male may be dissuaded from mounting by her actions. The male can also become overexcited and overheated if his overtures are repeatedly unsuccessful. Instead, after an initial period for introductions and flirting, the female should be held for the male. It is normal for dogs to remain "tied" for 10 to 30 minutes. Keep both of them cool and calm during this time.

For optimal chances of conception, repeat the breeding every other day until the female will no longer accept the male. Be sure to keep her away from other males during this time; dogs are not known for their fidelity! The AKC will not register litters fathered by more than one sire.

Lady in Waiting

Now you have two months to wait and plan. Gradually increase and change the expectant mother's food to a high-quality puppy food as time progresses. Keep her in shape, as a well-conditioned dog will have fewer problems whelping, even if a C-section is necessary. At the end of the first month, your veterinarian may be able to feel the developing puppies, but this is not always accurate. Two encouraging signs of pregnancy that might appear at around this same time are a clear mucous discharge from the vagina and enlarged, pink nipples. If at any time the discharge is not clear, seek veterinary attention at once.

Avoid letting her run up and down stairs, especially after the first month. When carrying her, be sure that you are not putting pressure on her abdomen. Do not give any medication without your veterinarian's advice. Your pregnant female should be isolated from strange dogs beginning three weeks before her due date; exposure to certain viruses during that time does not allow her to develop sufficient immunity to pass to her puppies, and can result in the loss of the litter.

False Pregnancy

Many females are prone to *false pregnancies*, a condition in which the breasts become slightly enlarged and

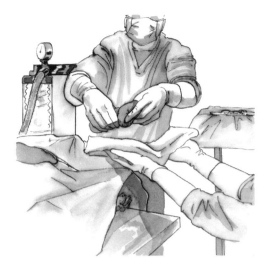

Be prepared for a C-section. Make sure that your veterinarian is experienced with Pekingese anesthesia and available on her due date.

may even have some milk. Pronounced cases involving large amounts of milk production, weight gain, and even nesting behavior and the adoption of certain toys as "babies" may be unhealthy and should be checked by your veterinarian. Some can be so convincing that even experienced breeders have thought their bitch was in whelp until she failed to deliver puppies!

How to Manage Special Deliveries

If you have never assisted at a small dog whelping, talk to your veterinarian or an experienced Peke breeder about what to expect. Discuss the signs of dystocia and procedures involved in a C-section. Consider an elective C-section as an option.

The Whelping Box

You should prepare a whelping box that will double as a nursery, and place it in a warm, quiet room. You can use the bottom of a plastic dog cage, a large cat litter pan, or a sturdy clean

The tiny sleeve females should be cherished, but never bred.

cardboard box. The sides should be high enough so that the young pups cannot get out, but low enough so that the mother can get over them without scraping her hanging nipples. You will find it much easier to assist her during whelping if you place the box on a

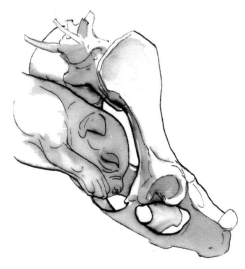

Normal presentation position in the birth canal.

tabletop, but when you cannot monitor her comings and goings, you must place it on the floor. Place the box on a rug or other insulating material, and line the inside with newspaper (preferably blank newsprint, and never colored sections), or preferably washable towels or blankets. Don't use indoor/outdoor carpeting, which tends to interact with urine in such a way as to irritate pups' skin.

The whelping kit should include:
• whelping box
• rectal thermometer
• many towels and washcloths
• nasal aspirator
• scissors
• dental floss
• heating pad or heat lamp
• warm box in which to place newborns while awaiting the arrival of any siblings
• bitch's milk replacement and nursing bottles with small-animal nipples attached
• highlighted whelping instructions
• emergency phone numbers

Preparing for Delivery

A few days before the due date, clip the hair from and thoroughly wash the areas around the vulva and the breasts. You should be counting the days from the first breeding carefully. While 63 days is the average canine gestation time, there is some variability, with small dogs tending to be somewhat early rather than late. In a 1975 study of gestation lengths in various breeds, Pekingese actually had the shortest pregnancies, averaging 61.4 days. A more accurate prediction can be made from counting the days from the first day of diestrus during the estrus cycle. This day can be pinpointed by your veterinarian, but you must begin the procedure near the beginning of her season.

You can get about 12 hours advance notice by charting the expectant mother's temperature starting around the fifty-sixth day; when her temperature drops to about 98°F (36.7°C) and remains there, make plans to stay home because labor should begin within 12 hours. Warm the whelping box to 80°F (26.7°C), and prepare for a long night. She will become more restless, refuse to eat, and repeatedly demand to go out. Make her as comfortable as possible and do not let her go outside alone where she might have a puppy. If you opted for a C-section, call your veterinarian at once so that you can make plans. Don't give her food or water before surgery.

Delivery

The natural birth of puppies is messy, so at this point you should remove any blankets you wish to save. As labor becomes more intense, she may scratch and bite at her bedding. The puppies are preceded by a water bag. Once this has burst, the first puppy should be born soon. As each baby is born, help the mother clear its face so it can breathe. In brachycephalic breeds, it is best for you to tie off the umbilical cord about 0.75 inch (19 mm) from the puppy with dental floss, and then cut it on the side away from the pup. If you can't tie the cord, crush the cord with hemostats or sterilized pliers, then cut it with scissors, keeping the crushed area between the pup and the cut. The crushing action prevents the cord from bleeding. Each puppy should be followed by an afterbirth, which the dam will try to eat. Allow her to eat one as they contain important hormones affecting milk production, but eating too many may give her diarrhea. You must count the placentas to make absolutely sure that none was retained in her; retained placentas can cause serious infection. Dry the puppy and place it on the mother's nipple to nurse. You may have to help it by opening its mouth and

Whelping Emergencies

You may have a whelping emergency if:
• More than 24 hours have passed since the dam's temperature dropped without the onset of contractions.
• More than two hours of intermittent contractions have passed without progressing to hard, forceful contractions.
• More than 30 minutes of strong contractions have passed without producing a puppy.
• More than 15 minutes have passed since part of a puppy protruded through the vulva and the puppy makes no progress.
• Large amounts of blood are passed during whelping. The normal color fluid is dark green to black.

Never allow a dam in trouble to continue unaided. She may need a Caesarean to save her life, and the longer it is put off, the poorer the chances of survival for her and her puppies will be.

A proud mother with her litter—one precious Pekingese.

85

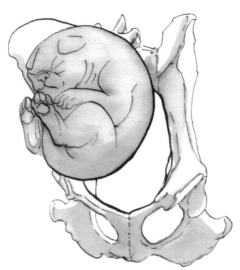

Dystocia resulting from a stuck puppy, in this case due to an overly large pup and abnormal position in the birth canal. A Caesarean section is essential.

squeezing a bit of milk into it. When the dam begins to strain to produce the next puppy, remove the first one to your temporary box warmed to 90°F (32.2°C).

Pekingese have small litters, and you may have only one puppy to deliver. Pups from such litters have a tendency to be larger than pups from large litters, and may be more likely to need a C-section for delivery. A prenatal ultrasound or radiograph in the last week of pregnancy can tell you ahead of time how many pups to expect. Data compiled from over 100 Peke litters indicated a typical litter size of three pups, with a maximum litter size of six.

It is not always easy to tell when the last puppy is born. If you have any doubts, have your veterinarian check her (you should bring her and the puppies for a post-birth check the next day anyway). It is normal for the dam to have a dark bloody or green vaginal discharge (called *Lochia*) for a week or two after the birth, but any signs of infection or foul odor associated with it is cause for immediate concern.

Postnatal Care

Monitor the nursing puppies to make sure they are getting milk. Pups with cleft palates will have milk bubbling out of their nostrils as they attempt to nurse. Some pups must be helped onto the dam's nipples; some dam's nipples are too large to fit in a pup's mouth. You should weigh each puppy daily on a gram or ounce scale to make sure that it is gaining weight. If not, ask your veterinarian about supplemental feeding.

Puppies cannot regulate their body temperature, and chilling can quickly result in death. This is especially critical for small breeds. The dam is understandably reluctant to leave them at first; you should place them in a warm box and encourage the dam to go out to her toilet area on a regular schedule. Use a heat lamp or heating pad to maintain the pup's environment at 85 to 90°F (29.4°C–32.2°C) for the first week, 80°F (26.7°C) for the second week, and 75°F (23.9°C) for the third and fourth weeks. Never feed a chilled puppy, except for a few drops of sugar water. Take care not to overheat the dam in your efforts to warm the pups.

Sometimes the dam's breasts become hard, swollen, or painful, indicating mastitis. Warm compresses can help her feel more comfortable, but if pus and blood is mixed with the milk, you will need to prevent the pups from nursing from those nipples and your veterinarian will probably prescribe antibiotics. This will necessitate artificially nursing the puppies so that they do not ingest antibiotic-containing milk.

In cases of infections, mastitis, or eclampsia, you may have to wean the puppies early. By fitting the mother with a "body suit," such as a sock or sweater sleeve with four leg holes, she can stay with the pups without letting them nurse.

Pekingese Pediatrics

Peke puppies are born with pink noses and eye rims that gradually turn dark beginning a few days after birth. If you elect to remove dewclaws, it should be done at about three days of age, however, many Peke breeders leave the dewclaws intact.

The puppies' eyes will open starting around 10 days of age, and their ears around two weeks. This age marks the beginning of rapid mental and physical growth. They will attempt to walk at two weeks of age. Be sure to give them solid footing (*not* slippery newspaper!). A "swimmer" is a puppy that cannot get its feet under itself and lies flat on its belly. Ask your veterinarian how to hobble the legs to assist it in standing. Such pups can develop normally if you give them some help.

The dam will usually begin to wean her pups by four to six weeks of age; smaller pups may need to stay with her longer. At around three weeks, you can introduce the puppies to food; baby food or baby cereal or dry dog food mixed with water and put through the blender is a good starter. They may lick it off your finger or you may have to put their noses in it. No matter what technique you use, be prepared to declare the feeding arena a major disaster area by the time the meal is over. Puppies seem to think they can best eat with their feet!

A Good Home for Life

After about six weeks of age, it is important that the puppies meet people so that they are well socialized, but this does not mean that they need to be exposed to a constant stream of new faces. Young puppies are irresistible, and your house may become the newest tourist attraction on the block, but don't let the puppies be overhandled, and don't allow the mother to become stressed by onlookers. Talk to your veterinarian about your puppies' vaccination schedule and visitors who could bring contagious diseases with them.

Placing the Puppies

There are two ways to place puppies: the ethical way and the unethical way. The unethical way is easy—sell each pup to the first comer for whatever you can get, and as soon as it leaves your house, wipe your hands of it. Don't think about the new owner who may not have a clue about raising a dog, who may think a Pekingese will be a fine outdoor watchdog, who is simply desperate for a Christmas present for the kids but really has no desire to keep it past the time they tire of it, or who wants a little money-maker that will be a puppy machine living in a cage until it dies of neglect. Yes, the unethical way is easy, until you try to sleep at night, every night for the next 12 years or so, as you lay awake wondering what fate you sealed for the little being who trusted you to care about its future.

The ethical way is initially more difficult, but will be easier if you have quality puppies with which to attract quality homes. If you have a quality breeding, word of mouth within the Pekingese world and at dog shows will be your best advertisement, but you can supplement with ads in dog magazines, and in various newspapers. You must play detective in ascertaining if prospective buyers have the sort of home in which you would be comfortable placing a puppy. One breeder relates that she evaluates prospective buyers by whether, if she had to give up the mother dog, she could be confident that this person would provide a good home for her. Once a sale has been made, the ethical breeder maintains contact with the puppy owner,

Their futures are in your hands.

and finally, the ethical breeder agrees that no matter what the age and whatever the reason, if the new owner can no longer keep the dog, it is always welcome back at its birthplace. If you can't make the commitment to be an ethical breeder, please don't be a breeder at all.

It may take time, but you can find a good home. Of course, after a while it may become obvious that the good home you find is your own!

The Proudest Pekingese

Pekes on Parade

The Pekingese has been one of the most consistently popular show dogs in history. Amidst the barking, tail-wagging dogs dancing for bits of liver, the Pekingese stands out as above it all. While other breeds race around the ring, the Peke strolls leisurely with the attitude that the show will just have to wait until it has taken its sweet time getting around the ring. Pekingese quality is so consistently high that competition can be extremely tough, so if you think you might want to try showing, be careful to take your time choosing the very best available dog. If you plan to breed your Pekingese, you should plan to compete in conformation in order to demonstrate to others that your dog is as perfect as you know it is.

Show Ring Greats

At the end of a dog show, one dog alone among the thousands competing stands undefeated—the Best in Show (BIS) winner. To win one such award is a coveted and remarkable achievement. Ch. Chik T'Sun of Caversham won over 100 Best in Shows, and held the record for many years for the top winning BIS dog of any breed in America. Among his supreme awards was the ultimate: BIS at Westminster, America's most prestigious dog event. Remarkably, two other Pekes have also won this highest honor in dogdom: Ch. St. Aubrey Dragonora of Elsdon and Ch. Wendessa Crown Prince. Who will be the next?

Be forewarned that care of the show dog's coat is not like caring for the average pet. It must be kept matt-free at all times. When a tangle occurs, it must be meticulously combed out with an effort to save each and every little hair. The serious show Peke can't go hiking in the woods or rolling in autumn leaves or swimming in a muddy lake. In fact, even carpet fibers can break hairs. The long hairs of the ears, tail, and britches may be wrapped in waxpaper secured by tiny rubber bands for protection.

Don't be surprised if it takes you a year or more to find a good show Peke; part of this time will be spent learning the standard (see pages 15–18), studying the breed, and talking with breeders. The *Orient Express*

The show Peke should walk happily and confidently on lead.

is a magazine devoted to the Pekingese, with an emphasis upon show Pekes, and is an absolute necessity in your quest. It's best to get your show Peke from a successful breeder, preferably one located fairly close to you. This way the breeder can help show you how to groom and prepare your dog for the ring, and give you tips on showing it.

The breeder should also be able to give you an honest opinion about your Peke's good and bad points, and its chances of success in the ring. As long as your Pekingese has no disqualifying faults (weight over 14 pounds [6.4 kg] or absence of two normally descended testicles in the scrotum) or is not spayed or neutered, you can show it, but if your Peke isn't really show quality, most breeders would prefer that you not show it. It's sometimes hard to win with your first show prospect, but you will still learn a lot about the show world and be better prepared in the event that you would like to show your next Peke.

Breathtaking on the move, the show Peke is evaluated for its distinctive rolling, yet smooth, gait.

In the Ring

Once in the show ring, the judge examines each Pekingese from head to tail and ranks them in accordance to their adherence to the official breed standard. Although the Peke has a reputation as a "head breed" (meaning that it is judged heavily on the conformation and expression of its head and face), there is far more to a good Peke than a perfect head. The judge must also consider the dog's coat, temperament, bone structure, and movement. The show Peke must be able to stand posed on a table without showing resentment or shyness when the judge examines it. It must walk around the ring to exhibit its distinctive rolling gait. The judge may pick the dog up to evaluate its weight. Remember that the Peke should be surprisingly heavy for its appearance.

There are professional handlers who will show your dog for you and probably win more often than you would; however, there is nothing like the thrill of winning when you are on the other end of the lead!

Contact your local kennel or even obedience club and find out if they have handling classes, or when the next match will be held. Matches are informal events where everybody's learning: puppies, handlers, even the judges. Don't take either a win or a loss at a match too seriously; in fact, even at a regular show remember that it is just one judge's opinion.

Show Points

At a real AKC show, each time a judge chooses your dog as the best dog of its sex that is not already a Champion, it wins up to five points, depending on how many dogs it defeats. To become an AKC Champion (CH), your Peke must win 15 points including two majors (defeating enough dogs to win three to five points at a time).

AKC Classes

You may enter any class for which your dog is eligible: Puppy, Novice, American Bred, Bred by Exhibitor, or Open. The Best of Breed classes are for dogs that are already Champions. Before entering, you should contact the AKC and ask for the free dog show regulation pamphlet, which will explain the requirements for each class. Your dog must be entered about three weeks before the show date, and you will need to get a Premium list and entry form from the appropriate show superintendent (their addresses are available from the AKC or most dog magazines).

Pekes are one of the few breeds in which open classes may be divided by weight.

At all-breed shows the division is:
• under 8 pounds (3.6 kg) if 12 months old or over
• 8 pounds (3.6 kg) and over (and under 8 pounds (3.6 kg) if less than 12 months old)

At specialty shows and some larger all-breed shows, the division is:
• under 6 pounds (2.7 kg) if 12 months old or over
• 6 pounds (2.7 kg) and under 8 pounds (3.6 kg) if 12 months or over
• 8 pounds (3.6 kg) and over (and under 8 pounds (3.6 kg) if less than 12 months old)

Because Pekes are so much a true family member, it can hurt to have your beloved dog placed last in its class. Just be sure that your Peke doesn't catch on, and always treat your dog like a Best in Show winner, whether it wins a blue ribbon or no ribbon at all. To survive as a conformation competitor, you must be able to separate your own ego and self-esteem from your dog. You must also not allow your dog's ability to win in the ring cloud your perception of your dog's true worth in its primary role—that of friend and companion.

The Heeling Pekingese

If your Peke is more than just another pretty face, you may wish to enter an obedience trial, where your little genius can earn degrees attesting to its mastery of various levels of obedience. You and your dog will have to prove yourselves in front of a judge at three different obedience trials in order to officially have an obedience title become part of your dog's name.

You plan on training your Pekingese the commands "heel," "sit," "down," "come," and "stay" for use in everyday life. Add the "stand for exam," and your dog will have the basic skills necessary to earn the AKC Companion Dog (CD) title. The AKC will send you a free pamphlet describing obedience trial regulations (see address on page 94).

Specifically, the AKC CD title requires the dog to:

1. Heel on lead, sitting automatically each time you stop, negotiating right,

Not all Pekes can bring home a treasure trove of trophies, but all deserve a chance to be named Best in Home.

left, and about turns without guidance from you, and changing to a faster and slower pace.

2. Heel in a figure eight around two people, still on lead.

3. Stand still off lead 6 feet (1.8 m) away from you and allow a judge to touch it.

4. Do the exercises in number 1, except off lead.

5. Come to you when called from 20 feet (6.1 m) away, and then return to heel position on command.

6. Stay in a sitting position with a group of other dogs, while you are 20 feet (6.1 m) away, for one minute.

7. Stay in a down position with the same group while you are 20 feet (6.1 m) away, for three minutes.

Each exercise has points assigned to it, and points are deducted for the inevitable imperfections. In all but the "heel" commands, you can give a command only one time, and in no cases can you touch, speak to, physically guide, correct, praise, or do anything except give the dog's name, followed by the command during that exercise.

As the judge feels for correct body structure, the handler makes sure that his dog is happy and looks its best.

No food may be carried into the ring. You must pass each individual exercise to qualify, and to earn the degree, you must qualify three times. The AKC will send a free rulebook to you on request.

Higher degrees of Companion Dog Excellent (CDX) or Utility Dog (UD) and Utility Dog Excellent (UDX) also require retrieving, jumping, hand signals, and scent discrimination. The OTCH degree is an Obedience Trial Champion; these are given only to dogs with UDs that outscore many other UD dogs in many, many trials. If you are at an obedience trial and see that an OTCH dog of any breed is entered, take the time to watch it go through its paces. The first OTCH Pekingese earned the title in 1995— OTCH Gidget to the Rescue, a Peke that was rescued from an animal shelter.

If you enter competition with your Pekingese, remember this as your Golden Rule: Companion Dog means just that—being upset at your dog because it "messed up" defeats the purpose of obedience as a way of promoting a harmonious partnership between trainer and dog. Failing a trial, in the scope of life, is an insignificant event. Never let a ribbon or a few points become more important than a trusting relationship with your companion. Besides, your Pekingese will forgive you for the times *you* mess up!

The Good Pekingese Citizen

In order to formally recognize dogs that behave in public, the AKC offers the Canine Good Citizen (CGC) certificate. To earn this title your Pekingese must pass the following exercises:

• Accepting a friendly stranger who greets you
• Sitting politely for petting by a stranger
• Allowing a stranger to pet and groom it

- Walking politely on a loose lead
- Walking through a crowd on a lead
- Sitting and lying down on command and staying in place while on a 20-foot (6.1 m) line
- Calming down after play
- Reacting politely to another dog
- Reacting calmly to distractions
- Remaining calmly when tied for three minutes in the owner's absence, under supervision by a stranger

The CGC is perhaps the most important title your Peke can earn. The most magnificent champion in the show or obedience ring is no credit to its breed if it is not a good public citizen in the real world.

The Healing Pekingese

Pekes can bring joy into your life; have you ever thought of sharing? As more of the population becomes elderly and either unable to care for or keep a pet, the result is particularly sad for lonely people who may have relied upon the companionship of a pet throughout most of their independent years. Studies have shown that pet ownership increases life expectancy, and petting animals can lower blood pressure. In recent years, nursing home residents have come to look forward to visits by dogs, including Pekingese. These dogs must be meticulously well mannered and well groomed; to be registered as a Certified Therapy Dog, a dog must demonstrate that it will act in an obedient, outgoing, gentle manner to strangers. The eye-catching Peke, with its calm personality and small size, is a natural for people who may

The Pekingese—always number one in its owner's eyes and heart.

not appreciate being overwhelmed by a licking clown. A friendly Peke could make a big difference in a lonely person's day.

Although Pekingese have proved they can make their mark in many areas of competition and social work, the most important role of any Pekingese is that of pet dog supreme. As you marvel at the many nuances of this living oriental treasure in your living room, you will understand fully why this unique breed has developed the most loyal worshippers in dogdom. The Pekingese, show dog extraordinaire, companion at home, partner in adventure, and oriental treasure. No wonder it is considered a big dog in a little body.

Useful Addresses and Literature

Organizations

The American Kennel Club
  51 Madison Avenue
  New York, New York 10038
  212-696-8200

AKC Registration
  5580 Centerview Drive, Suite 200
  Raleigh, North Carolina 27606-3390

The Pekingese Club of America
(address changes periodically)
  Mrs. Leoni Marie Schultz, Secretary
  Rt. #1, Box 321
  Bergton, Virginia 22811

Pekingese Rescue
(address changes periodically)
  I. Louis Harden, Chairperson
  Pasadena, Maryland
  410-255-2166

Orthopedic Foundation for Animals
  2300 Nifong Blvd
  Columbia, Missouri 65201
  314-442-0418

Home Again Microchip Service
  1-800-LONELY-ONE

Magazines

The Orient Express
  8848 Beverly Hills
  Lakeland, Florida 33809-1604
  941-858-3839

Dog Fancy
  P.O. Box 53264
  Boulder, Colorado 80322-3264
  303-666-8504

Dogs USA Annual
  P.O. Box 55811
  Boulder, Colorado 80322-5811
  303-786-7652

Dog World
  29 North Wacker Drive
  Chicago, Illinois 60606-3298
  312-726-2802

Books

Denlinger, Milo. *The Complete Pekingese*. Silver Spring: Denlinger's, 1957.

Godden, Rumer. *The Butterfly Lions: The Story of the Pekingese in History, Legend, and Art*. New York: Viking Press, 1978.

Hill, Herminie Warner. *Pekingese*. London: Foyle, 1970.

Quigley, Dorothy. *The Quigley Book of the Pekingese*. New York: Howell, 1964.

Index